THE
MAGDALENE
LEGACY

THE MAGDALENE LEGACY

*Exploring the Wounded
Icon of Sexuality*

Sandra M. Rushing

BERGIN & GARVEY
Westport, Connecticut • London

Library of Congress Cataloging-in-Publication Data

Rushing, Sandra M.
    The Magdalene legacy: exploring the wounded icon of sexuality /
    Sandra M. Rushing
        p.   cm.
    Includes bibliographical references (p.   ) and index.
    ISBN 0–89789–388–3 (alk. paper)
        1. Woman (Christian theology).   2. Mary Magdalene, Saint.   3. Women
    in Christianity.   4. Sex—Religious aspects—Christianity.
    I. Title.
    BT704.R87   1994
    230′.082—dc20   93–40160

British Library Cataloguing in Publication Data is available.

Library of Congress Catalog Card Number: 93–40160
ISBN: 0–89789–388–3

First published in 1994

Bergin & Garvey, 88 Post Road West, Westport, CT 06881
An imprint of Greenwood Publishing Group, Inc.

Printed in the United States of America

The paper used in this book complies with the
Permanent Paper Standard issued by the National
Information Standards Organization (Z39.48–1984).

10 9 8 7 6 5 4 3 2 1

I dedicate this book to my daughter, Deborah Jean McCrowell, a woman whose wisdom belies her years, and whose encouragement has been vital to my continued study, of sociology, of psychology, and of theology. I have learned much from her courageous questioning of my old beliefs and assumptions. She has taught me much about my own individual frailty. When I risk speaking for a collective of women, I speak from a place which acknowledges the enhancing influence she has had on my life, and the way in which she has enlarged my ability to own the parts of myself which are ultimately and completely human. I hope that this book, in which she has shared, will bring a blessing into her life.

Contents

Acknowledgments   ix
1. Introduction   1
2. The Historical Perspective   9
3. A Look Backward--To Mary Magdalene   43
4. The Misogyny of Modern Theology   63
5. Rushing Toward Body Denial   97
6. The Legacy of Women Ascetics   107
7. Jesus and Archetypal Wholeness   129
8. Jesus, Mary Magdalene, and Projection   147
9. Seeking a Transcendent Body/Spirit   161
10. Reflections Upon the Now   177
Appendix A   189
Appendix B   201
Bibliography   205
Index   215

Contents

Acknowledgments

I am grateful for my friend, colleague, and mentor, Dr. Gail Roen, who pushed me to a larger awareness of my internal woundedness, my own authenticity, and my vital spiritual energy. With her help and the therapeutic, analytical work I completed with Dr. Ken Peterson, I began my journey toward wholeness. That journey continues with this book, even as it began the day I was born and was enhanced when I had the courage to publish my first book of poetry.

I want to express my gratitude to many others whose words have given me both comfort and courage as I have walked along this path. The works of Marion

Woodman (herself the daughter of a minister) were the healing balm for much of the wounding I needed to salve before I could own my spiritual authenticity. Her books have each touched me at a particular place in the journey when I most needed it. While I have striven to give Marion Woodman credit wherever her concepts have been used, those very concepts are now so much a part of my being that I suspect I have used them without adequate credit. I hope that whatever I have written is a reflection of the healing that I have realized as I have read Marion's words. I have learned so much from her writing, as well as the writing of my favorite woman theologian, Ann Belford Ulanov.

Ann Belford Ulanov has helped me to bridge the gap between my ongoing interest in the psychological theory of Carl Jung and my more recent study of theology. Barry Ulanov read this manuscript and offered critical advice on its final preparation. His affirming words of endorsement and long distance encouragement came at a time when I needed just such an affirmation. Thank you, Barry. I express my appreciation to Virgil and Margot Cruz, who were the first to spur me forward in my study of this subject, and whose endorsement brings meaning to all my hours of New Testament study.

I am grateful, as well, for numerous others from whom I have learned so much; they include Walter Brueggemann, Nancy Qualls-Corbett, John Dourley, Edward Edinger, Elaine Pagels, Sylvia Perera, Letty Russell, Rosemary Radford Ruether, John Sanford, Bishop John Shelby Spong, and many others too numerous to mention.

My friends Meri-Li Douglas, Karen Paul, and Marilee Olson Houg have shared the journey of women entering the ministry. They know the seminary experience; they know the ego-dying aspects of the gauntlet toward ordination. I am grateful for their friendship, their caring for me in my darkest hours, their love and companionship when I needed it most. Eric and Lisa Nielsen were two loving people who entered my life at seminary. Their down-to-earth mid-western style was a wonderful counterpart to my "Southern woman" one. We shared laughter and tears, graduation, and the birth of their daughter Sarah together; all of that I will not forget.

My editor, Dr. Lynn Flint, has been encouraging and affirming with me when I did not even know enough to ask the right questions! She has journeyed with me as I made my way along the path toward publication, nudging me gently when I needed nudging, and speaking to me with the voice of wisdom as I worked to meet deadlines. Her warm nurturance along the way has been invaluable, and I thank her for it.

One special woman from my congregation completed the final editing of this book during my last weeks in the parish. Inge Lundh embodies the best of my understanding of what an elder in the Presbyterian Church can be, and I am gratified that she was a participant in the final preparation of this book.

I am grateful for the proofreading that my friend Kathy Rion completed. Her strong ability to plow through this tedious task was a tremendous help to me. I appreciate the kind help of Tom Raisbeck, who taught me how to use a new word-processing package in order to complete the camera-ready copy of this manuscript.

My husband, (the Reverend Doctor) Phillips Leedom Carr, is the partner who stands by my side while I work long hours in the parish, and whose presence in my life is surely God-given. He provides an informed theological reaction to my questions regarding both accepted canon and extra-canonical works. He is a sounding board as I walk into the text and, with trepidation and faith, look for new meaning and nuance.

But beyond that, he comes to hand me a sandwich and a glass of milk when I have stayed at the computer straight through the meal hour. He slips silently into my office and embraces me with the strong arms of a horseman, one who has taken me back to the smell and taste and spirit of horses. He urges me to leave my work to go for a ride on the wonderful horse I bought at his urging; I do not "do exercise" very well and he knows it!

With him I know that love is a sacred experience between two people who are each on separate, unique psychic journeys, and yet are joined at a profound level of understanding. For that love, come late to my life, I am grateful; for Phillips I am grateful.

THE
MAGDALENE
LEGACY

1

Introduction

"Your body is the harp of your soul..."
                                    --Kahlil Gibran, *The Prophet*[1]

This study has multi-faceted beginnings. Somehow it
began with the affirmations of a Virginia country preacher whose extreme halitosis was offputting for many of
his parishioners, but whose nurturing encouragement
honored my toddling yearnings for the divine. It was
strengthened by another country preacher whose speech
impediment made him a less-than-excellent example of
one whose "pulpit presence" is awe-inspiring. Perhaps it
reached a zenith in the Fraumuenster Church in Zurich, a church whose name means "women's cloister,"
where I beheld the magnificent windows designed by
Marc Chagall. The central window, entitled "Christ
Glorified," shows the figure of Jesus the Christ in a

vivid kelly green, symbolizing the color of spring, of resurrection, of crucifixion and rebirth in ascension.

When I think of the resurrected "Christ Glorified" in Zurich, I also think of the twelve stained glass windows designed by Marc Chagall for the Hadassah Hospital in Ein Karem, Israel; each of the windows depicts one of the twelve tribes of Israel.

The juxtaposition of the images depicted within these windows seems like a fitting metaphor, a proper beginning, for this study. It cannot set aside the Judaic pieces of my own faith which are deeply rooted and grounded in the theology of the Old Testament, even as it must honor the New Testament realities of my Christianity. But it strives to add a new coloration and texture to that Christianity, one which I hope will provide a different insight and spirit for women who may have struggled to connect with their God in the same ways as I. Beyond my own experience, I want to touch in some way all the angry women I have encountered who have and are working in the institutional church. As we walk toward a new day globally, the church lags behind, even as it gives lip service to egalitarian ideals.

When I try to remember the fragments and pieces which became an impetus for this study, I cannot forget one of my first encounters with a young woman minister in the district governing unit of my denomination who railed at me in anger over a detail of a financial report prepared in another office (never crossing my desk). I remember the profound sense of bewilderment I experienced as I tried to respond to her anger. It took years for me to look back and achieve a retrospective (and yet limited) understanding of that anger. It was not until I had experienced the underlying and unconsciously punitive aspects of being a woman who was running the gauntlet for ordination within my denomination that I truly understood it, at least in part.

Another fragment (and a further impetus for this study) came from a woman minister in her farewell embrace before I left the secure support of my network of friends to go to seminary. As she held me fiercely in a good-bye hug, she exclaimed, "Oh God, I hope they don't break your spirit at seminary; they break the spirit of so many women."

I understand so well what she meant as I experience the day-to-day assumptions of Western theology, assumptions which will be explored in this study. The anger many women experience both as lay leaders and as members of a male-dominated clergy will be honored in this study, for the long-standing grief it continues to manifest. It is an unresolved anger which has spiraled downward into unremitting grief. Even when some women have been bold enough to express their authentic anger, that anger has not been honored. It has been ignored by a male-dominated majority in both academic and ecclesiastical arenas, or it has been denigrated as "tripe" by "radical feminists" who have misplaced notions about themselves and religion in general. So many women, so much anger, so much grief, and from a depression that cries out for a hearing, the women who are clergy--and the women who have a strong, innate sense of their own wounded spirituality and their sexuality, still wait for someone to hear. This book is presented in the hope of addressing a necessary healing for the wounding in *both* genders. That healing must have divine inspiration and a human understanding that the critical piece of our finite existence is one of relational connectedness, both to each other and to our God.

I emphasize that this book, while including theological research, is not one which is intended as an exegetical (interpretation of scripture) exercise. My methodology has not been one of traditional, accepted exegesis, with the linear, rational parameters implied by such a methodology. I have written out of my authentic experience. I do not intend for this work to be viewed as either a literary or historical criticism of accepted canon. I am not an historian, but I am a sociologist and a theologian, with a strong interest in Jungian psychology. My methodology is more akin to that of early writers of the *Midrashim*, who took the Scripture of their Jewish faith and struggled with it, argued with it, asked questions of it, and ultimately reinterpreted it for their time and place in the history of the world.

While the quotes used in this context are intended to anchor and clarify my premise regarding the underlying causes for the distortion of women's spirituality/sexuality in today's culture, they are not ones which present the whole character or personality of those who are quoted. The people who are used as examples, or are quoted in the context of this study, lived full, complex lives in an entirely different geographical and cultural milieu. I present here my experience (and the witnessed experience of others) as a personal statement of authentic faith, not as a pronouncement of a universal truth or as the superior or exclusive reading of the material which is quoted.

There is still another fragment in my own spiritual journey; it is a remembered admonition from two different men, both of whom had left their ordination and the church for the success offered in another field. Each told me, without equivocation, I was making a mistake to begin my work on a Master of Divinity degree because, "the Church is a dead institution, the secular world has more attraction and it is only a question of time before the Church dies." I was urged to study for a doctorate in sociology instead. If I had believed these men were accurate in their assessment, I would not be writing these words.

There is more than a kernel of truth in their dire pronouncements about the Church, in that I believe the old dogmas and doctrines are dying a much-needed death, albeit a slow and agonizing one. That death is prolonged by the sometimes desperate, sometimes successful attempts at resuscitation of ancient and outmoded theories which are not only inapplicable in today's world, but are actually destructive for it. But the intensive care efforts are valiant; the ecclesiastical atmosphere is clouded with the escaping oxygen applied in an effort to maintain the archaic authoritarianism of a dead generation, and the verbal battle cries of those who would ignore a plea for new images are not easily stifled or ignored.

I do not speak for myself alone, but rather, for a collective who longs for authentic connectedness to a real and interpersonal God. As I give voice to the anger and grief of women, in particular, I do so with steadfast respect for the particularity of each one's unique pain and soul-felt honor for the ways in which it has been both repressed and expressed.

On April 27, 1989, Dr. Alan Culpepper, J. B. Harrison Professor of New Testament and Associate Dean of Ph.D. and Th.M. Studies at Southern Baptist Theological Seminary (Louisville, KY), was the guest speaker for one of my seminary classes. I consider myself fortunate because this professor, and respected Biblical scholar, gave me an enhanced insight regarding Biblical criticism as it has evolved historically. In consulting the notes I took that day, one particular quote stands out. Dr. Culpepper said that new interpretations of Biblical texts need to hear the inner voice of the narrative, with its implicit themes, in order to minimize distortion because, "What is not stated is *not* insignificant, but rather may reflect an irony, an unspoken setting, a cultural assumption, or a *deliberate* exclusion." I believe that the last of these is at work in the canonical writings I will explore.   Dr. Culpepper also indicated that sociological facets of Biblical stories lend themselves to an enriched interpretation not otherwise possible.   I believe a psychological interpretation of the Biblical text can further enhance previous methodologies.

With these assumptions in place, I intend to use the image of Mary Magdalene to explore the inherited roles of women in today's world.   By using her story as the underlying paradigm for this book, I will discuss the historical heritage women are now struggling to address, both in the secular arena and in the church.   I will use the theory of Swiss psychiatrist and psychoanalyst Carl Jung, and the sociological theory of Thorstein Veblen, to show how deeply held psychological and sociological patterns have a remarkable impact upon the lives of modern women and men.

I can think of no better way to state my understanding of what this book is about than to quote from Dr. Carl Jung.   Writing in 1933, Carl Jung indicated:

> ... ideas which are hailed as truths have something peculiar to themselves.   Although they come into being at a definite time, they are and have always been timeless; they arise from that realm of procreative, psychic life out of which the ephemeral mind of the single human being grows like a plant that blossoms, bears fruit and seed, and then withers and dies.

Ideas spring from a source that is not
contained within one man's personal life.
We do not create them; they create us.[2]

Such is the source of this book. The ideas themselves
created the impetus for it, and for me.
Throughout this book, certain terms which origi-
nated with Jung will be used. They are: the feminine
or "anima," the masculine or "animus," and the "shadow." On a deep level of the unconscious psyche,
below that structured, precise level of the conscious
mind where cultural norms are honored, and below the
ego standing as a protective obstacle to their awareness,
lie the shadow and archetypal levels of the unconscious.

In the first of these, the *personal unconscious*, we
store the repressed, societally rejected material acquired during our lifetimes. Because we are consciously unaware of this repressed psychic material, it is then
projected outward onto others who represent our shadow. This material passes back and forth between
individuals of the same gender and is quite often accompanied by obvious and overt physical energy released in the projection. The dynamics of male domination in the cultural, economic, and theological arenas
lie deep within the shadow and the archetypal levels of
the psyche.

At the archetypal level, the deepest level of the
unconscious, is material which is instinctual and primitive, representing thousands of years of social patterns,
ones which have been distorted by those cultural norms
or societal expedients held at the conscious level of the
psyche. At this level we find the anima or feminine
archetype and the masculine or animus archetype (a-
long with other identifiable archetypal patterns). The
anima can be described as a quality of authentic yield-

ing relatedness, an eros/soul aspect of the psyche. The animus, as the masculine counterpart, is defined as the logos aspect, one of linear action potentiality.

Both women and men hold these archetypes deep within the psyche, but the Western culture does not recognize or give credence to their existence or (more importantly) the unconscious stress related to a failure to own them as visceral aspects of the personality. Because the shadow level of the psyche is one which both individuals, and the collective of both genders, maintain in an unconscious way, the resulting contra-sexual tension is profoundly powerful. It is the very unconscious nature of this phenomenon which creates its strength.

Notes

1. Kahlil Gibran, *The Prophet* (New York: Alfred A. Knopf, 1983), 72.

2. C. G. Jung, *Modern Man in Search of a Soul* (New York: Harcourt Brace Jovanovich, 1933), 115.

2

The Historical Perspective

"We have carved Ishtar from solid marble..."
--Kahlil Gibran, *Secrets of the Heart*[1]

In the last year of his life (1961), Dr. Carl Jung wrote:

> Modern man does not understand how
> much his "rationalism" (which has de-
> stroyed his capacity to respond to num-
> inous symbols and ideas) has put him at
> the mercy of the psychic "underworld." He
> has freed himself from "superstition" ...,
> but in the process he has lost his spiritual
> values to a positively dangerous degree.
> His moral and spiritual tradition has dis-
> integrated, and he is now paying the price
> for this break-up in world-wide disorienta-

> tion and dissociation. ... But we have
> never really understood what we have
> lost, for our spiritual leaders unfortunately
> were more interested in protecting their
> institutions than in understanding the
> mystery that symbols present. ... We have
> stripped all things of their mystery and
> numinosity; nothing is holy any longer.[2]

Jung could have been writing in 1994, instead of (more than) thirty years earlier. Many leaders of the church continue to focus upon ways to protect this social institution, as an institution and as it has been historically understood, instead of enlarging their vision to incorporate newer understandings and theological perspectives. Jung's predictions regarding cultural and social deterioration have much to do with the continuing absence of numinous feminine metaphors with which women can identify. The theological, cultural, and economic arenas continue to be dominated by unhealthy patristic symbolism.

I suggest that an image is available to us, an image that will allow women and men to reconnect and recapture a balanced perspective of spirituality (and thus sexuality). That image is embodied in Mary Magdalene, and this book will address her transformative image as a prototype for those who intuitively know that spirituality and sexuality are deeply and acutely interwoven. She stands as an ignored icon who can teach modern Christians much about their faith. She offers us a superb legacy, one we have needed in a rather desperate way.

Jung believed that "matter," as it has been defined by the scientific community, has been distorted. From that distortion, we have lost all understanding of its earlier, soul-level aspects of, and relationship with, our being. When matter is reduced to a purely rational concept, when it is only explored and dissected and viewed under the precise microscope of those who claim to be capable of purely objective opinions, then the soul is robbed of its place in the world, for the soul resides within matter, and matter is the substance of human frailty and subjectivity. By reducing matter to the limited understandings of the human imagination and the intellect, the God whom we worship is limited in the same way. That God becomes a power hungry authoritarian ruler of the universe, one without feeling, one who surely lacks a female counterpart. From that one-sided, and limited, view the church has functioned for two thousand years.[3]

These are the dynamics which have occurred in social institutions, dynamics which have devalued or distorted the feminine or "Mother Earth," and secularized the spirit or "our Father" into an intellectual god of technology. These changes have allowed the Western culture to deify that which is precise, linear, and intellectual, and to denigrate that which is illogical, mysterious, and relational. It is a process of suppressing the feminine in order to magnify the masculine. It is a process of killing the soul, the anima, while distorting the animus, the masculine partner to the soul; the centered, wise partner is distorted into an image not dissimilar from that of a multi-national corporate chief executive officer.

The masculine and the patriarchy cannot be equated. The patriarchy is a manifestation of a juvenile masculine, an expression of a "stunted masculine," one that "feels itself impotent, both in relation to the feminine and to other men."[4] The patriarchy is driven by an overweening power principle. That abuse of power is derived from fear, "operating out of anxiety, not confidence." This is the masculine "fixated at an immature level."[5] Addressing the impact of the patriarchy does not mean elevating the feminine, while subordinating the masculine. The task is to celebrate the potent intentionality of the masculine, not reduce its authentic power. But, at the same time, the relational feeling which is feminine must also be celebrated, for through it we connect with the true anima or soul within. Then we can better utilize the animus. The authentic and integrated masculine, the animus, is that internal aspect of both genders which pushes us to accomplish specific goals, that equips us to complete even difficult tasks and projects.[6]

The institutional church has, however, manifested the negative masculine. My personal experience in one denomination, the Presbyterian Church, U.S.A., has been one in which I have been forced to recognize the cultural contamination that is inherent in the institutional church. By unconsciously adhering to cultural "norms," the Presbyterian Church, U.S.A. has taken each step of the process for ordination (to the ministry of the Word and Sacrament) and distorted it into a technological gauntlet of agony: a linear and intellectual process from which the mystery and numinosity has been stripped.

While on the one hand there is a powerful unconscious urge toward transcendent ritual and initiation, the primitive facets of that urge are denied and manipulated into a "head trip." The male-dominated process denies the shadow aspects of this gauntlet of agony, protesting that those who survive the process have proved their suitability through the process, itself. But, all these factors are part of a larger, more insidious picture. The church, and its denominations, as much as it might claim otherwise, mirrors the culture. In that mirroring, the church also lays claim to the same problems and the same understandings of itself and its people. The processes for addressing those problems have been developed by a culture that is itself contaminated. Thus, both the culture and the church reflect an unconscious misunderstanding of self in relationship with God and others.

Even as (some of the) mainline denominations struggle with images of God as female, the most recent translation of the canon (the New Revised Standard Version) is symbolic of the collective unconscious determination to protect the status quo. Although language for humans is inclusive, God is still presented as a masculine figure; (i.e., "So God created humankind in his image, in the image of God he created them; male and female he created them."). Such unconscious imagery is rooted in our inherited understandings of a God figure.

The historical transformation of pastoral egalitarian societies into warrior patriarchal societies became the definitive turning point for the ways in which people would both envision God and relate to each other. That change is remarkably evident, even in a society which exists thousands of years after the fact. Riane Eisler, an attorney and futurist, in her book entitled *The Chalice and the Blade*, traces the cultural origins of Goddess-worshipping societies and indicates that they were not confined to a specific geographic region, but rather occurred in various places at roughly the same time.

She, along with a number of anthropologists, like André Leroi-Gourhan, and archaeologists, like James Mellaart and Marija Gimbutas, suggest that these archaeological digs yield cultural information which was distorted (whether consciously or unconsciously) by previous (male) scientists. Research using C-14 or radiocarbon dating has led the scientific community to reassess past historical assumptions regarding the evolution of certain cultures and their levels of civilization at the time of their termination. Marija Gimbutas writes regarding these findings:

> Old Europeans never tried to live in inconvenient places such as high, steep hills, as did the later Indo-Europeans who built hill forts in inaccessible places and frequently surrounded their hill sites with cyclopean stone walls. Old European locations were chosen for their beautiful setting, good water and soil, and availability of animal pastures, but not for their defensive value.[8]

When earlier, more egalitarian societies set the standards by which they would chose their places of living, they did so, not from a male-oriented one of defense nor from an assumption of war, but in order to maintain a style of life that was spiritual and pastoral in nature. They lived in harmony with the earth and thus with the internal Great Mother. Gimbutas continues:

> A division of labor between the sexes is indicated, but not a superiority of either. In the 53-grave cemetery of Vinca, hardly any difference in wealth of equipment was discernable between male and female graves. ... In respect for the role of women in the society, the Vinca evidence suggests an egalitarian and clearly non-

patriarchal society. The same can be
adduced of the Varna society; I can see
no ranking along a patriarchal masculine-
feminine value scale.[9]

Again, the evidence shows that these societies were
aware of cooperative forms of governing and had no
need to elevate one gender over another. But, this
kind of living pattern, this kind of understanding of the
self in relationship with others, was destroyed by the
warrior societies.

Both Gimbutas and Eisler discuss the finding
that these digs from early pastoral societies yield no
evidence of warrior activity. The peoples of these
earlier cultures did not elevate aggression and violence
to a level of "national defense;" it was not a priority.
The innate spiritual aspects of life were more important
than defending the territory in which one lived. Eisler
writes:

> One of the most striking things about
> Neolithic art is what it does *not* depict.
> For what a people do not depict in their
> art can tell us as much about them as
> what they do. In sharp contrast to later
> art, a theme notable for its absence from
> Neolithic art is imagery idealizing armed
> might, cruelty, and violence-based power.
> There are here no images of "noble war-
> riors" or scenes of battles.[10]

Eisler indicates that these same findings show an absence of great stocks of weapons for defense or purposes of aggression. Nor did these cultures have mili-
tary fortifications constructed as protection against the

armed aggression of neighboring tribes. Archaeologists who study this data must then assume that these Neolithic peoples were primarily motivated by, and lived in, peace.

Prior to the definitive work by Gimbutas, V. Gordon Childe, a European historian, had written:

> Competition for land assumed a bellicose character, and weapons such as battle-axes became specialized for warfare. ... The consequent preponderance of the male members of the communities may account for the general disappearance of female figurines, now no more in evidence. The old ideology has been changed. That may reflect a change from a matrilineal to patrilineal organization of society.[11]

Childe's characterization of this change as from "matrilineal to patrilineal" is disputed by Gimbutas, Mellaart, and Leroi-Gourhan (all of whom interpret the archaeological data to support a premise that these societies were more or less egalitarian in structure). But, the *critical factor* in this change is that barbaric invasions destroy these peaceable cultures, replacing them with, or radically changing them to, warrior societies which emphasize the power model. Eisler points out that men, who are more powerful physically and more aggressively violent than their smaller female counterparts, then become the ones who determine the societal norms and the course of history. The mode of governing becomes "more hierarchic and authoritarian," and the status of women is changed forever after. Eisler continues:

At the same time the Goddess herself
gradually becomes merely the wife or
consort of male deities, who with their
new symbolizations of power as destructive weapons or thunderbolts are now
supreme. In sum, through the gradual
process of both social and ideological
transformation ... the story of civilization
now becomes the familiar bloody span
from Sumer to ourselves; the story of
violence and domination.[12]

That "bloody span from Sumer to ourselves" is carried
more unconsciously, than it is carried at a level of conscious awareness. It has become a part of our cultural
assumptions; it forms the basis for the expenditure of
millions of dollars in defense funds every year. Our
collective inability to hold a vision of peace (as an
alternative to power-driven war) is paralleled by our
individual inability to envision a divine internal god/-
dess who loves us without harsh judgment, but who
calls us to more conscious awarenesses of our own individual soul reality.

Rosemary Radford Ruether also describes the
change to male-dominated societies and its parallel in
the change of religious deities which no longer embody
or encompass a diversity of personality characteristics,
when she writes:

The Greeks had divided the ancient
Goddess, who was both virgin and mother, protector and warrior, into separate
types: Athena, the virgin warrior; Artemis, the virgin huntress; Hera, the
nagging wife of Zeus, and Aphrodite, the

love Goddess. These types represent the
severing of the Goddess from earlier
wholeness and cultic power and her transformation by the literary imagination of
patriarchal society.[13]

This change creates the fragmentation of what Carl
Jung referred to as "archetypal patterns" in the collective unconscious. Just as St. Paul in his writings had
separated the psyche/soul from the body: "For the
desires of the flesh are against the Spirit, and the desires of the Spirit are against the flesh; for these are
opposed to each other,"[14] so, too, is the balanced, whole
perspective of a creator Mother Goddess with both
benevolent and malevolent characteristics lost to later
generations. With this separation of female imagery
from the spiritual realm comes a concurrent denigration
of the female as a species of human being. Women are
taken out of the plane of the spiritual and relegated to
a subordinate and subservient status.

The sociological theory of Thorstein Veblen can
be a way of understanding the sociological dynamics
that arise from this dichotomous split between female
and male. Whereas Jung referred to archetypal patterns, Veblen refers to conventional or common patterns of thinking as "habits of the mind." He believed
that:

> ... habits of the mind are not mentally
> stored in a random or haphazard way but,
> rather, in consistency with the overall
> nature of human mental abilities; fur-
> thermore, they are organized around a
> people's particular, usual, and typical
> activities. They thus come to support,

cognitively and emotionally, typical ways of behaving and oppose violations of the usual. In other words, a people's habits of the mind form the basis of cultural norms. Thus culturally normative views of right and wrong, acceptable and unacceptable, are grounded in mental habits that have emerged from repetitive productive activity. Once cultural norms emerge, they both form the basic common stock of knowledge of a people and are strengthened as they are passed down to later generations through socialization.[15]

Whether we view them as unconscious archetypal patterns or *as habits of the mind*, the resultant cultural norms have been dramatically changed from their primitive origins. Women who are now striving to establish an egalitarian role in society have inherited the institutions which emerged after this gender-related societal change. The image of a feminine side of God is lost to women who are members of the Western society. Merlin Stone discusses the additional impact of the Judeo-Christian influence and its destruction of the feminine from the realm of the spiritual:

The female religion, especially after the earlier invasions, appears to have assimilated the male deities into the older worship and the Goddess survived as the popular religion of the people for thousands of years after the initial invasions. By the time of Marduk and Ashur of the sixteenth century B.C., Her position had

been greatly lowered in Mesopotamia.
But it was upon the last assaults by the
Hebrews and eventually by the Christians
of the first centuries after Christ that the
religion was finally suppressed and nearly
forgotten.[16]

I believe Stone is correct when she asserts: "the orders
for the destruction of the religion of the Goddess were
built into the very canons and laws of the male religions that replaced it."[17] The legal stipulations set forth
in the Old Testament books of Deuteronomy and
Leviticus make remarkable sense if one understands the
underlying, hidden agenda. That hidden agenda had
two primary and yet unpublic faces. They were power
and control. By stating that men were the ones who
must be honored, even obeyed, and by implication,
declaring that women were therefore the ones who
would be obedient, all power and control of the family,
the society, and the direction of a given culture, was
then lodged within the masculine domain.

From these barbaric invasions, not only is the
religion associated with a female Goddess suppressed
or destroyed, but certain concepts of morality now
become the accepted cultural norm. Spirituality and
sexuality are defined by the male dominated, warrior-
bound culture. Women become targets for projections
of a negative sensuality on the one hand, while becoming mere pieces of male-owned property on the other.
Their "morality" is defined by cultural *habits of the
mind*, and they are judged by a different standard than
their male counterparts.

The issue of male dominance had a certain
vitriolic quality about it that can be quite horrifying if
viewed in perspective with past practices of Goddess-

worshipping cultures. Both Hebrew law and later Christian scholarly pronouncements reveal this underlying trait. As an example:

> If a man meets a virgin who is not be-
> trothed, and seizes her and lies with her,
> and they are found, then the man who lay
> with her shall give to the father of the
> young woman fifty shekels of silver, and
> she shall be his wife, because he has
> violated her; he may not put her away all
> his days.[18]

This Old Testament reference from the Pentateuch is only one of many laws regulating the sexual practices of the Hebrew people. What is startling and quite ugly about it (and many other similar Judaic laws) is the no-win societal position of the woman. Here her reward for being raped is a life sentence of marriage to her rapist. Who is rewarded? Her father! Her economic value is set at fifty shekels and her rapist is not prosecuted or punished in any way; but rather, his reward for a violent sexual act is a lifelong marriage to the person he has violated.

Later Christian leaders revealed their unconscious assumptions and projections in their negative views of women. These "fathers of the church" are infamous for the very nature of their misogynistic thinking, thinking which was clearly the norm of their day, thinking which has permeated the direction of the church. Religious reformer Martin Luther is quoted as saying the following:

> Men have broad and large chests and
> small and narrow hips and more under-

standing than women who have but small
and narrow chests and broad hips, to the
end that they should remain at home, sit
still, keep house and bear and bring up
children. If women get tired and die of
bearing, there is no harm in that; let them
die as long as they bear; they were made
for that.[19]

In these words, Luther revealed the evidence of archetypal patterns, or generational imprints, assuming
male superiority and female inferiority. The women
who "die as long as they bear" were disposable repro-
ductive machines, ones which men had every right to
control. It is important to note here, that Luther's
archetypal patterns (or *habits of the mind*) are not just
an indication of the Christian influence, but a cumula-
tive imprint of both Judaic and Christian belief, all
evolving out of barbarism.

Those *habits of the mind* are critical to our
understanding of both the assumptions of theological
belief and the dynamics of cultural stagnation. Thorstein Veblen's sociological theory on the habits of the
mind had three basic concepts:

1.   They occur without rational reflection
     (they are assumed and not questioned in
     the course of such reflection).

2.   They appear to be in congruity with and,
     in fact, form the basis of commonsense
     understanding among the people in ques-
     tion.

3.   They are resistant to change and tend to

persist for a time even after the material conditions that gave rise to them have disappeared.[20]

Contemporary cultural norms regarding the status of women have evolved out of the barbaric annihilation of cultures which revered women. Even though these invasions occurred thousands of years ago, the cultural dynamics they have created are "resistant to change and tend to persist." Nevertheless, the "material conditions that gave rise to them have disappeared."

Because our society is one that prides itself on thinking, on intellectual, rational solutions to problems and on technological deities, we have lost touch with the intuitive, instinctual, and the primitive qualities necessary for holistic grounding at a psychic level. While the culture has emphasized the masculine (what Jung would define as the structured, precise and direct), it has suppressed and devalued the feminine (what Jung viewed as the instinctual, yielding and mystical). However, these gender-specific, stereotypical attributes evolved after the time when the divine was held in the container that was female. The visceral qualities of sensuality associated with Goddess worship have been forbidden, and the transcendence of primitive ritual has been pushed into an artificial atmosphere (like a drive-in church) or sublimated into unconscious patterns (like the binging and purging of bulimia).

The earlier tradition regarding the sacred quality of childbirth was dramatically changed by the Judaic law of the Old Testament, *The Torah* (and its commentary, *The Talmud*). Now, women were excluded from the office of priestess; the Goddess was destroyed, and even the process of birth was defiled. This tainted, dirty perception has only been dispelled in recent years.

Even today Orthodox Jews, particularly Hasidic Jews, adhere to the anachronistic edicts of the priests who created this law. For example, here is another excerpt from the canon:

> The Lord said to Moses, "Say to the people of Israel, If a woman conceives, and bears a male child, then she shall be unclean seven days; as at the time of her menstruation she shall be unclean. And on the eighth day the flesh of his foreskin shall be circumcised. Then she shall continue for thirty-three days in the blood of her purifying; she shall not touch any hallowed thing, nor come into the sanctuary, until the days of her purifying are completed. But if she bears a female child, then she shall be unclean two weeks, as in her menstruation; and she shall continue in the blood of her purifying for sixty-six days.[21]

The difference in the period of time in which the mother was/is to be declared "unclean" is just another manifestation of the stratification of the genders and the subordinate status assigned to females under Judaic law. The fact that she is considered to be unclean twice as long after giving birth to a daughter is an indication of the same kind of feeling exhibited by Talmudic commentators who later make pronouncements like, "Women are naturally inclined to witchcraft," and, "The more women there are, the more witchcraft there will be."[22]

The very blessings which are part of the fiber of Jewish thought were, by implication, reserved only for male children. One of the rabbis who wrote in the Talmud declared, "What is the interpretation of 'all things' in the Scripture? 'The Lord blessed Abraham in all things'? That he had no daughter!"[23] In the same text another rabbi, while less negatively emphatic, wrote, "May the Lord bless thee with sons, and keep thee from daughters because they need careful guarding."[24]

After the birth of her child, the Toraic law stipulated that the woman must "atone" by bringing a "sin offering" to the priest. It cannot go unnoticed that those who wrote this law were priests! All these sin offerings kept these men in good style; they were freed for scholarly pursuits. The exclusion of the women from the inner place of worship at this time kept them from participating in another sacred ritual, that of the circumcision of the superior male child, "superior" because a daughter had no ritual which celebrated her birth. Instead, her mother was the recipient of a more punitive measure of her uncleanness. Those who give life are now regarded as unclean and sinful.

Lis Harris, in her book entitled *Holy Days*, writes of the world of the Hasidic family; it is a world circumscribed by the laws and traditions of orthodox Judaism. She is critical of the separation of the genders dictated by the Torah and the Talmud and describes in vivid detail the jumble of bodies in the women's balcony section of the synagogue. These women, invisible behind the plexiglass shield of their assigned section, still adhere to the laws set forth in the canon.

These same Jewish women, while living in the contemporary concrete world that is Brooklyn, also participate in the ritual bath or *mikvah* prescribed for Jewish women after their menstrual period ends. Harris writes: "On Friday afternoon the men go to the *mikvah*, or ritual bath, to purify themselves for the Sabbath."[25] In contrast, women are required to immerse themselves in the *mikvah* after menstruation and before sexual intercourse, because of the ancient Judaic belief that sexual intercourse is sacred. "Men shed whatever taint they may have acquired in their weekday workaday world when they immerse themselves before the Sabbath; women purify themselves as an acknowledgement of the holiness of sex."[26]

This contrast between the male immersion before the Sabbath, or participation in the spiritual, and female immersion before sexual intercourse, or participation in the physical, serves as an example of Judaic law (and practice) which separates the female from a holistic participation in the spiritual. This pattern is still a part of our contemporary assumptions; it is part of a perceived cultural norm, a *habit of the mind*.

The rituals of Judaism, not unlike the rituals of Christianity, have evolved from those practiced by earlier polytheistic cultures. During the time of King Josiah, the Hebrews had cult priestesses who lived next to the temple and were weavers of hangings for the sacred grove.[27] These holy women participated in a ritual bath which was symbolically hymen-renewing and allowed them to carry the perpetual designation of "virgins." This ritual bath was designed to renew that virginity, even though, as part of their sacred duties as temple priestesses these women engaged in sexual intercourse with the men who came to worship at the temple.[28] The early leaders of Israel, adopting this practice, modified its connotation to honor their patriarchal social system and forever after designated women as unclean at certain times.

Christianity has neither honored women more, nor recognized their status in a more egalitarian way.

The Christian inheritors of the Hebrew tradition had much to say about the status of women. Women who enter contemporary and institutional ministry do so knowing that the historical tradition of a literal interpretation of the canon is against them. From the New Testament we read: "Let a woman learn in silence with all submissiveness. I permit no woman to teach or to have authority over men; she is to keep silent. For Adam was formed first, then Eve; and Adam was not deceived, but the woman was deceived and became a transgressor."[29] These words form a part of that historical tradition; they are a powerful reminder of old assumptions of a norm.

Here the author heaps onto the heads of Christian women the same burden of guilt carried by generations of their Judaic predecessors. Eve is blamed for the sinful nature of all humankind. But, in addition to assessing blame and assigning it to women, the writer, in saying "Adam was not deceived," absolved men of any responsibility for what Augustine and the church term "original sin."

Widows were instructed in the following way: "A wife is bound to her husband as long as he lives. If the husband dies, she is free to be married to whom she wishes, only in the Lord. But in my judgment, she is happier if she remains as she is. And I think that I have the Spirit of God."[30]

The author here, the apostle Paul, reveals his own inflated ego and then goes on to instruct this church, as well, about allowing women to speak: "As in all the churches of the saints, the women should keep silence in the churches. For they are not permitted to speak, but should be subordinate, as even the law says. If there is anything they desire to know, let them ask their husbands at home, for it is shameful for a woman to speak in church.[31]

Here Paul is quite precise in his instructions and refers to the stipulations of "the law" as he articulates these restrictions. Even though he matures into a Christian who is capable of setting aside the (Old Testament) law for the understanding of the "new covenant," Paul reflects the firmly implanted *habits of the mind* of his day and age. Paul is a Pharisee through and through, and his assumptions bear witness to his orthodox training and understanding of his world, as a Jew. Sadly, these same assumptions continue to mirror the beliefs of many in the institutional church. Paul sets up the continuing pattern of male domination with his admonition:

> But I want you to understand that the head of every man is Christ, the head of a woman is her husband, and the head of Christ is God. Any man who prays or prophesies with his head covered dishonors his head, but any woman who prays or prophesies with her head unveiled dishonors her head--it is the same as if her head were shaven. For if a woman will not veil herself, then she should cut off her hair; but if it is disgraceful for a woman to be shorn or shaven, let her wear a veil. For a man ought not to cover his head, since he is the image and glory of God; but woman is the glory of man. (For man was not made from woman, but woman from man. Neither was man created for woman, but woman for man.)[32]

Literal translationists still love this passage; it is quoted ad nauseam as a reason for the subjugation of women. Those denominations which still hold women in subordinate positions of powerlessness rely on these kinds of passages to defend their positions.

Paul is not the only great Christian leader who is guilty of misogynistic attitudes (as evidenced by the earlier quote from Martin Luther in this text). St. John Chrysostom, fourth century Christian orator who served as Patriarch of Constantinople said, "Men suffer a thousand evils from having to look at women; the beauty of women is the greatest snare."[33] According to Walter Map, Canon of St. Paul's Archdiocese of Lincoln and Hereford, "Even the very good woman, who is rarer than the phoenix, cannot be loved without the loathsome bitterness of fear and worry and constant unhappiness."[34]

Out of such archetypal imprinting, the American nation was established and its social structures implanted in the soil of a new land. The historic status and ultimate political power enjoyed by (or denied to) women in the United States was born out of laws evolving from barbarity, economic domination, and gender stratification. The earliest settlers carried with them these unconscious and primitive concepts of cultural norms, these *habits of the mind.*

Imagine the dismay with which the English colonists viewed the roles of women in the various Indian tribes. Historians have recorded that women who were members of American Indian tribes were accorded places of prominence in these tribes, not just as mothers, wives, and cooks, but as recognized political leaders, who wielded concomitant power in the Indian society. While many of the plains Indian tribes did not elect women to the position of chief, in the Lakota tribe, women voted and took an active part in council deliberations. Their Anglo-Saxon and African-American counterparts were not allowed to vote until 1920, after almost one hundred years of suffrage activity by women across the nation.

The Lakota frowned upon women going into battle, not because they were viewed as too weak to participate, but rather because they were the "keepers of the race." The women were regarded as the protectors of the morals and mores of the people. This Lakota belief was symbolized in the pow-wow, where the women formed the outer circle around the men, who would dance in the inner circle, symbolizing their role as the physical protectors of the people. At the very center of these two circles of dancers were the drummers, who symbolized the Great Spirit or God.

The Cheyenne tribe, allies of the Lakota, reflected a difference in tribal understandings of women's roles. Cheyenne women went into battle as warriors, fighting side by side with the men. In the Battle of the Rosebud, which preceded the Battle of the Little Big Horn, the Lakota (led by Crazy Horse) and the Cheyenne fought together against the U. S. Cavalry, commanded by General George Crook. As the battle waxed and waned, a Cheyenne warrior was wounded and fell between the lines of Indian warriors and the soldiers. His sister charged out between the two lines, picked her brother up, and carried him to safety on her horse.[35]

Some of the Algonquin tribes elected women to the position of chief, but one of the more famous Native-American women leaders was the Lady of Cofitachique, who ruled over a number of villages in the southeast (in an area that now comprises the western part of South Carolina). The women of the Iroquois tribes also had leadership roles in their largely agrarian societies.[36] As a woman who grew up in the authoritarian household of a Virginia "gentlemen farmer," I find it ironic that "the most powerful female rulers were found in what is now the southeastern United States."[37] Into the doorway of my memory steps an image of my father, with his face crimson and the carotid artery on the side of his neck pulsing in rage, screaming at me, "You can't go to seminary and become a preacher; girls don't do that!" When he had regained some measure of composure, he commented, "You can go away to college, since you have an academic scholarship, but you will not study to be a preacher."

In reaction I ran away from home and married a boy who was a stranger. I did not take advantage of my academic scholarship to attend what was then Montreat College. The power which my father's authority held within, and over, my psyche was not broken until more than ten years after he had died. I did not enroll at a university until I was forty-six years old. Yet, I am not different from so many other women who matured to womanhood in the southeastern United States. The social dynamics of "Southern" expectations, regarding Southern women, have created generations of closet alcoholics. These bright, but subordinated, women "belong" to the males who dominate the clans in this anachronistic setting.

The Puritans, who settled the opposite end of the east coast, creating the northern counterpart to the Southern Woman, also stressed a Biblical role for women. Religion held a primary position in structuring these new colonies and two historical codes of the day, the Mayflower Compact and the Fundamental Orders of Connecticut, were interlaced with Christian dogma.

Norton, et al., indicate that: "All households were taxed to ... pay ministers' salaries. Massachusetts' BODY OF LAWS AND LIBERTIES incorporated regulations drawn from Old Testament scriptures into the legal code of the colony."[38] The law of the tooth and claw was again embraced and its basic tenets were intertwined into the first legal codes drawn in the history of this nation. It was very much a part of the texture of these new colonies and any deviation from it was viewed with alarm.

One woman who created great upheaval was Anne Marbury Hutchinson. She was considered a dangerous threat to Puritan orthodoxy because she taught her followers that they could communicate directly with God and be assured of salvation. Charges were brought against her in the General Court of Massachusetts in 1637. She successfully defended herself for two days against a man of no mean repute, John Winthrop, himself. But, "in an unguarded moment late in the second day, Hutchinson declared that God had spoken to her 'by an immediate revelation.' That heretical assertion assured her banishment; she and her family, along with some faithful followers, were exiled to Rhode Island."[39]

Perhaps the Puritan leaders of the day could have tolerated Anne Hutchinson's theological concepts had she not been a woman, but her gender got in the way. Those who were in positions of authority saw Ann Hutchinson as a two-edged threat. Not only was she audacious enough to defy the "religious orthodoxy" of the day; she also had the audacity to step outside her culturally defined gender role.[40]

Those colonies originally settled by English subjects typically adhered to the restrictions of British common law. Its particular (or peculiar) decrees included stipulations which prohibited married women from drafting wills,[41] from selling or purchasing land in the colony,[42] or making contracts.[43] Furthermore, colonial men "expected their wives to defer to their judgment." If a woman owned property before her marriage, it reverted to her husband when they wed; whatever she earned, all her wages, could be legally claimed by her husband; and no matter how many children she birthed, they were bound by law to a father who could exercise "absolute control."[44]

That control determined the degree to which girl children were allowed any exposure to the intellectual. While boys were educated with a view toward preparation for college, their sisters were only instructed in areas related to a presumed form of gentility. The girls were taught how to embroider, as an example, or how to play the piano, or even to dance, but all with a view toward preparation for marriage, not the higher education represented by colleges and universities. Such education for girls was regarded as unnecessary.[45]

The stage was then set for upholding gender tension and male domination. As the United States progressed into the industrial age, the role of wife and mother was emphasized and glorified, but that emphasis and glorification had a stunted quality about it. It allowed the woman to delude herself about the power of her position in a culture that continued to deny her any real power, in a culture that demanded her acquiescence at every angle.

With the Industrial Revolution, women were relegated to the home and its environs, where they were expected to set the tone for a family unit which represented the ultimate shelter from the crass environment of the business and industrial arena. Thus was born the notion of a "woman's sphere," that place where the wife and mother was the moral leader of a micro-cosmic piece of the larger societal whole. Yet, the woman held no real power, except that which her husband delegated to her. On the contrary, the woman of the house was expected to be a paragon of "self-sacrifice," who taught her daughters to do likewise. Her sons, however, were expected to follow their father into the larger world of commerce and industry.[46] In creating a women's sphere, the culture then placed women in the paradoxical role of household goddess, in that:

> It was in Victorian times, that a 'lady' in the American sense, was defined by the distance between herself and the market-place. ... Paradoxically, it was from this worthless 'idleness' (often not idleness at all, but an endless round of unpaid house-hold chores), that women derived a new status and class. Middle class women, dependent on their husbands, were elevated to 'ladies' and considered superior to poor women who worked.[47]

Here women's purpose and esteem were linked to a glorious representation of idealized motherhood; women were supposed to hold themselves above the baseness of monetary compensation. Although on the one hand, their work in the home was priceless and too glorious to be measured in monetary terms; on the other hand, it was economically valueless, worth no-thing at all. This same skewed thinking is evident in political sound bites that glorify "family values" for a nation that has no consensus or definition of such values. Nevertheless, it is increasingly clear that both political parties in the United States are determined to

claim their definition as the "right" one.
This distortion of actual worth, and a continued glorification of antiquated gender roles, has created a socio-psychological phenomenon which excludes women from participation in both politics and the church. It is symptomatic of the psychic imprinting which women have inherited.
Margherita Rendel has written that historically male politicians have controlled the positions of power within the government and our political parties. That women would be incorporated into the hierarchy of this system is questioned, because women's concerns are viewed as "soft and unimportant," or even "unreal." Rendel writes:

> Paradoxically, it is the discipline's treatment of these differences which demonstrates the problem. What we see in the treatment of women is a symptom of a larger problem--a willingness to either avoid questions of power and justice by blaming the victims, or to substitute explanations based on social norms, while at the same time ignoring the political system's role in the maintenance of these norms.[48]

The paradox is not that easily addressed. The dichotomous nature of this phenomenon is more complex than understanding social or cultural norms. Its underlying power is not purely sociological in origin; it is locked in the primitive level of the collective psyche. The collective will strive both to protect and to maintain this norm, because the collective is relatively unconscious of the norm's existence in the first place. We cannot consciously address that which we have not brought to a cognitive level of awareness. The continuing discussions regarding legislation on abortion, spousal abuse, and appropriate penalties for those convicted of rape are an indication of the powerlessness of women in the political arena. But, the unconscious aspects of these issues are far more problematic, because they are still hidden within the archetypal levels of the collective psyche.

Because every facet of a woman's role is inherently linked to the phenomenon herein discussed, findings by political science researchers can be applied to areas related to theology and to the pursuit of a theological education. One of these components is "achievement orientation." Those who point to socialization patterns as an explanation for male dominance in the political arena, and in the church, go on to indicate that women lack the endurance and tenacity required for the rigorous schedules demanded of politicians and/or theologians.

Baxter and Lansing use the following quote from *The American Voter* as an example:

> It is the sense of political efficacy that ... differs more sharply and consistently between men and women. Men are more likely than women to feel they can cope with the complexities of politics ... to believe that their participation carries some weight in the political process. ... moralistic values about citizen participation in democratic government have been bred in women as in men, what *has been less adequately transmitted* to the women is a sense of some personal competence vis-

a-vis the political world.[49]

Thus, not only do women believe they lack the hardy qualities needed for a participation in politics (again, substitute theology or "the ministry"); they also believe they lack the ability to "cope with" its "complexities." It is not the actuality which stultifies and inhibits women, but rather it is what their psyches allow them to believe that creates the obstacle. But, their psychic assumptions are derived from cultural assumptions, and cultural assumptions are derived from the underlying *habits of the mind* which formed the culture.

Demographic gender patterns confirm that women are actually stronger than men. That elderly women greatly outnumber elderly men is a census-based statistical reality. But women, functioning out of unconscious restrictions, do not believe they have whatever is necessary to break out of this traditional mold.

So, too, women who are part of the institutional church find themselves in a similar dilemma. While they have been "given permission" (by the male-dominated hierarchies of the church) to enter the ranks of its clergy, they are still the recipients of unconscious projections related to their competence or ability to manage the work of a parish. Underlying these projections is an archetypal projection of distorted sexuality, and assumed incompetence, which colors the way they, as leaders, are perceived. Even as such projections occur, more and more men who are clergy, and lay leaders within the church, insist that their reactions and projections are not gender related. Yet, when one encounters such reactions and projections, one knows that Mary Magdalene is not alone; her modern counterparts are legion.

Notes

1. Kahlil Gibran, *Secrets of the Heart* (New York: Signet Books, 1947), 43.
2. C. G. Jung, *Man and His Symbols* (San Sebastian, Spain: Ferguson Publishing Co., 1964), 94. Here I am aware that Jung's language is not inclusive. While such exclusive language is troubling for the modern reader, Jung died before inclusive language had become a matter of conscious awareness. Even the grand old man, himself, had not reached a divine level of consciousness!
3. Ibid., 94-95.
4. Robert Moore, "Healing the Masculine" (Lecture given at the C. G. Jung Institute in Chicago, 1991).
5. Ibid.
6. Jungians Robert Moore and Marion Woodman emphasize this point in their lectures and in their writing. Too often the masculine and the patriarchy have been equated, with no understanding of the positive function of the masculine in the psyches of both genders.
7. Genesis 1:27, *The New Revised Standard Version of the Holy Bible* (Nashville: Thomas Nelson Publishers, 1990), 2.
8. Marija Gimbutas, *The Early Civilizations of Europe: A Monograph for Indo-European Studies* (Los Angeles: University of California Press, 1980), 17.
9. Gimbutas, *The Early Civilizations of Europe*, 32-33. The location of the Vinca dig is a site in Europe, fourteen miles east of Belgrade in the former nation state of Yugoslavia.
10. Riane Eisler, *The Chalice and The Blade* (San Francisco: Harper and Row, 1987), 17-18.

11. V. Gordon Childe, *The Dawn of European Civilization* (New York: Alfred Knopf, 1958), 109.

12. Eisler, *The Chalice and The Blade*, 53-54.

13. Rosemary Radford Ruether, *Woman Guides, Readings Toward a Feminist Theology* (Boston: Beacon Press, 1985), 6.

14. Galatians 5:17; *The New Oxford Annotated Bible* (New York: Oxford University Press, 1962), 1415.

15. Thorstein Veblen, edited by David Ashley and David Michael Orenstein, *Sociological Theory: Classic Statements* (Newton: Allyn & Bacon, Inc., 1985), 373-74.

16. Merlin Stone, *When God Was a Woman* (New York: Harcourt Brace Jovanovich, 1976), 68.

17. Ibid., 196.

18. Deuteronomy 22:28-29; *The New Oxford Annotated Bible*, 243-44.

19. Martin Luther quoted in Amaury Riencourt's *Sex and Power in History* (New York: Dell Publishing Co., 1974), 258.

20. Ashley & Orenstein, *Sociological Theory*, 373.

21. Leviticus 12:1-5; *The New Oxford Annotated Bible*, 135.

22. Julio Caro Baroja, *The World of Witches* (Chicago: University of Chicago Press, 1965), 80.

23. A. Cohen, *Everyman's Talmud* (New York: Schocken Books, 1975), 171.

24. Ibid.

25. Lis Harris, *Holy Days: The World of the Hasidic Family* (New York: MacMillan Publishing Co., 1985), 59.

26. Ibid., 137.

27. II Kings 23:7; *The New Oxford Annotated Bible*, 489.

28. E. O. G. Turville-Petre, *Myth and Religion* (New York: Holt, Rinehart and Winston, 1964), 236.

29. I Timothy 2:11-14; *The New Oxford Annotated Bible*, 1441-42.

30. I Corinthians 7:39-40; *The New Oxford Annotated Bible*, 1387.

31. I Corinthians 14:33-35; *The New Oxford Annotated Bible*, 1394.

32. I Corinthians 11:3-9; *The New Oxford Annotated Bible*, 1390.

33. St. John Chrysostom quoted in Bernard Murstein's *Love, Sex and Marriage Through the Ages* (New York: Springer Publishing Co., 1974), 160.

34. Walter Map quoted in Elizabeth Stanton's *The Original Feminist Attack on the Bible* (New York: Arno Press, 1974), 194.

35. This information was acquired in a telephone conversation with Art Raymond, of the Lakota tribe, retired Director of Indian Program Development at the University of North Dakota, Grand Forks, N D.

36. Mary Beth Norton, et al., *A People and a Nation* (Boston: Houghton Mifflin Co., 1986), 8.

37. Ibid.

38. Ibid., 34.

39. Ibid., 35-36.

40. Ibid., 36.

41. Ibid., 44.

42. Ibid., 54.

43. Ibid., 84.

44. Ibid.

45. Ibid., 89.

46. Ibid., 277.

47. Carol Hymowitz and Michael Weissman, *A History of Women in America* (New York: Bantam, 1978), 64.

48. Margherita Rendel, ed., *Women, Power, and Political Systems* (New York: St. Martins Press, 1981), 51.

49. Sandra Baxter and Marjorie Lansing, *Women and Politics* (Ann Arbor: The University of Michigan Press, 1980), 48. The emphasis is mine.

3

A Look Backward—To
Mary Magdalene

"(The one) who looks upon us through the eyes of God
will see our naked and essential reality."
                        --Kahlil Gibran, *Spiritual
                        Sayings of Kahlil Gibran*[1]

Mary Magdalene, a woman whose skimpy story is an
integral part of the New Testament narrative, is a
woman who has carried collective (cultural) projections
for thousands of years, projections which reflect the
complex nature of women's roles, and the societal
expedients which affect women's lives. She is the archetypal female in the imagery associated with her
sensuousness and sexuality, but she is stereotypical in
her "fallen Eve" imagery. But, the most distorted facet
of her portrayal is that of her spirituality. Biblical
scholars John McLintock and James Strong note that
Mary Magdalene is "one of the most interesting, but at
the same time most contradictorily interpreted charac-

ters in the New Testament."[2] This does not stop these same scholars from discounting the significance of the risen Christ's appearance to Mary Magdalene when they write:

> A careful comparison of the relative time of the several appearances of Christ on his resurrection makes it evident that the term "first" applied by Mark (xvi 9) to the appearance to Mary, must not be taken so strictly as to exclude the prior appearance to the other females who had accompanied her to the sepulchre.[3]

Here is reflected a sentiment (whether unconscious or otherwise) that cannot allow its authors to believe that Jesus would have appeared first to Mary Magdalene and not to his mother, Mary, who may have been one of the "other females." These authors, like many early Christian apologists, seem to believe it is necessary to protect the Virgin Mary's prominence, while discounting that of Mary Magdalene.

Early fathers of the church (and their successors), in their effort to explain the inexplicable, elevated Mary's actual Biblical role. No further mention of Mary, Jesus' mother, occurs in the New Testament after she is placed among the women at the foot of the cross in John's account of the crucifixion, except for a brief reference to her in Acts 1:14 (after the ascension of the resurrected Christ). Her lack of scriptural prominence, when compared to Mary Magdalene, led to attempts to reinterpret the deafening silence surrounding the Virgin Mary, by denying the actuality of the Magdalene's role in the life of Jesus.

These quotes from the same source mirror the

difficulty one encounters in researching Mary Magdalene. The early church, including the authors of the
New Testament Gospels, could not quite decide how to
portray Mary Magdalene. She is not easily set apart
from all the other New Testament Maries, who were
viable characters in their own right. She is the com-
posite essence of many other women who bear the
name Mary, and the deeds and misdeeds of more than
one Mary have been attributed to her.

As early as 1536, a Roman Catholic scholar,
Jacque Lefevre d'Etaples, provoked a huge stir when he
suggested that Mary Magdalene and Mary of Bethany
were not the same person. His study and its findings
were angrily debated and denounced; even though his
findings are now accepted by many theologians, the
tainted image of Mary Magdalene has not yet been
redeemed.[4]   Lefevre d'Etaples was punished for his
boldness; he was censured by the theological faculty of
the Sorbonne.

To find an accurate account of the "true" Biblical
Mary Magdalene is probably impossible, but is certainly
akin to embarking upon a Malekulaian labyrinth, one in
which the design is erased as one approaches. It is a
story which parallels that of most Biblical women, one
of only fragments and torn pieces, pieces that have
been distorted, altered, or never written.

In the course of this research, one is struck by
the differences between those statements and assumptions which are perceived as historically accurate by
male theologians and the more recent research by
women theologians. A European theological scholar,
Elisabeth Moltmann-Wendel, in differentiating between
Mary Magdalene, and Mary of Bethany, and the unnamed woman who anointed Jesus, writes, "The early
Christian Church fathers, e.g. Iranaeus, Origen, and

Chrysostom, were still unfamiliar with the identification of the three women of the Bible."[5] As a result, Moltmann-Wendel notes that Mary Magdalene's story has been distorted, creating "the greatest historical falsification in the West, in favor of patriarchalism, which had the most influence on the place of women in the church."[6]

Another scholar, Karl Künstle, believes Augustine was responsible for blurring the identities of these three women whose stories are depicted in the Gospels. He declared that Augustine was "responsible for the confusion between the three women, which was probably congenial to him for psychological reasons because it must have been a comfort for him that the Lord resorted so often to Mary of Bethany, although she had once, like him, been caught up in the toils of sexuality."[7] Moltmann-Wendel adds that the image of Mary Magdalene has been distorted by Western theologians who have "located sin one-sidedly and clearly in human corporeality, and specifically in woman."[8]

The Greek Orthodox church celebrated three feast days in commemoration of Mary of Bethany, Lazarus' sister, the unnamed woman who was labeled a sinner, and for Mary Magdalene, the first witness to Christ's resurrection. The Western church followed the interpretation of Pope Gregory the Great and combined these three feast days under the name of Mary Magdalene and celebrated one feast day in honor of the "passionate penitent" on July twenty-second.[9]

Mary Magdalene is seen as representative of the stereotypical sinful woman. She carries the resultant negative connotations of sexuality as sinful, and sensuality as lacking in spirituality. To test this (unconscious) projection, I mentioned this particular research project to a friend, a doctor who had grown up in the

Catholic tradition, and his bewildered response was, "Why in the world would you want to waste time writing about a woman who was a whore?" So this is the imagery which Mary Magdalene carries, imagery projected onto a woman who seems remarkably vivid even though she is mentioned only fourteen times in the New Testament.[10]

Like the collective need to project a national satanic projection onto the Soviet Union during the years after the end of World War II, the ecclesial collective has used Mary Magdalene as a convenient scapegoat figure. If she is carrying the passionate penitent projection, then those who preach and teach Christianity feel somehow absolved from responsibility for addressing their own internal and negative passions. But males are not alone in their projections onto Mary Magdalene. Denise Lardner Carmody writes: "Mary had loved Jesus while wretched and in her sins because he had dealt with her face to face, treated her kindly, affirmed her personhood, given her something worthy of her passionate love."[11]

What kinds of "wretched sins" has this woman committed to warrant the condescending pronouncements of theologians? How does she acquire this image? Demons! From Mark's account (Mark 16:9), as well as Luke's narrative (Luke 8:2), the Biblical reader will find that Mary Magdalene was "possessed by seven demons." How are these demons manifested? Apparently Mary Magdalene was epileptic or prone to a syndrome which carries the label "manic-depressive" in today's culture. One scholar notes:

> She was probably an epileptic, for epilepsy was commonly attributed to possession by evil spirits. This reference in Luke's

Gospel immediately follows the story of the sinful woman who anointed the feet of Jesus during a meal in the house of Simon the Pharisee. The tradition of the Church from early times identified Mary of Magdala with the woman living an immoral life in the city. Rightly or wrongly, Mary has become for all Christians the type of passionate penitent.[12]

There are two implications in viewing Mary Magdalene as a passionate penitent. One is that Mary, in her possession by demons, exhibited wanton, inordinate sexual behavior which could only be alleviated by spiritual healing. There is a morbid parallel to be found in modern psychiatry (which labels modern anomics as manic-depressives) in that one of the listed symptoms for applying this label is "excessive involvement in pleasurable activities (which have a high potential for painful consequences), e.g., the person engages in unrestrained buying sprees, *sexual indiscretions*, or foolish business investments."[13]

The other implication evolving out of this view of Mary Magdalene has been the undergirding of a Roman Catholic tradition, whereby penance retains a sacramental elevation. Here the penitent Magdalene was embraced over the centuries as an image of reconciliation by European Christians who were seeking a mediator. As this mediator, she is connected to the soul-level understandings of Christians who espoused her for this purpose. But in the Reformed tradition, Mary Magdalene becomes the historic example of a woman who has to be healed, cured of her sexual indiscretions.

This delineation is apparent in the dichotomy

which has been unconsciously created at an archetypal
level. Women, inheriting these dichotomous projections,
are thrust into an either/or position. Either they are
immoral and sexual or they are moral and spiritual, but
they cannot be both sexual and spiritual. The projection of this assumption onto women in ministry is part
of the dilemma for them. Many women entering the
ministry bear the tension and ambivalence of their
archetypal struggle to connect their spirituality and their
inherent sexuality. If they are single, any overt sexual
activity (outside the bounds of marriage) can be questioned, and/or viewed with alarm, by a potential calling
congregation. If they are married, and middle-aged,
any suggestion that they are overtly sexual and/or
sensuous can be deemed inappropriate for them as
clergy. The Biblical reader cannot discover anything
more than a cloudy image of the woman who was the
Magdalene, for:

> Mary of Magdala has been identified with
> the woman with the alabaster cruse who
> anointed Jesus in the house of Simon the
> Leper of Bethany, as recorded in Mark's
> and copied in Matthew's Gospel. All
> these anointings have their variations on
> the theme of the reformed sinner or
> passionate penitent, yet not one of them
> can be linked with the slightest degree of
> certainty with Mary of Magdala.[14]

Even though the projection continues, other Biblical
scholars have tried to correct this tainted image of
Mary Magdalene. For example, a 1911 edition of the
Bible Encyclopedia and Scriptural Dictionary has this

notation:

> Much wrong has been done to this in-
> dividual from imagining that she was the
> person spoken of by St. Luke in ch. vii:
> 39, but there is no evidence to support
> this opinion. ... How Mary Magdalene
> came to be identified with the person
> here mentioned, it is difficult to say; but
> such is the case, and accordingly she is
> generally regarded as having been a
> woman of depraved character. For such
> an inference, however, there appears to
> be no just ground whatever.[15]

While Biblical scholars have, for more than eighty
years, agreed that Mary Magdalene's story is one which
has been distorted, there is still little accuracy to be
found in writings about her. The definitive exception to
this can be found in the writings of Elisabeth Moltmann
-Wendel.

What did this Mary, whose distorted story became one of aberrant sexuality, look like? There is no
way of knowing from the references to her in the Bible.
But the projections of the collective imagination are
evident in the following: "We can be confident she was
a woman who walked erectly, even to the tomb, one
who was young and pretty, well-favored and warm-
hearted. The master painters depicted her with auburn
hair, a woman beautiful of face and form."[16]

The above description is typical in its presump-
tive notions regarding Mary Magdalene's youth and
beauty. But Elisabeth Moltmann-Wendel disagrees
with these assumptions, stating: "In male fantasies she
usually seems to be unmarried, young and beautiful.

But perhaps she was already aged, had a marriage behind her which provided the means with which she was able to help the Jesus movement, and showed traces of the illness which she had overcome. We do not know."[17] An accurate description of Mary Magdalene's physical appearance is impossible, "we do not know," nor will we ever know.

Depictions by ancient and medieval period artists, however, are still held in the collective imagination when images of Mary Magdalene are conjured. Artists who painted her face and figure on stone coffins, and who portrayed her (as the first witness to the resurrection) on ampullae, showed her, with hair flowing freely, carrying a vase in her arms.[18]   The vase, itself an ampulla, would have held the anointing oil and spices with which she intended to anoint the dead body of Jesus.

Whatever her appearance, Mary Magdalene is depicted as a woman who truly loved Jesus. Here the reader cannot fill in the gaps left by accepted canon, without turning to certain literature which has been historically labeled as "heretical." These heretical sources can be illuminating for just this purpose, and a number of theologians are currently using them to enhance the narrative of the accepted canon.

Quoting from the Gnostic *Gospel of Philip*, Elaine Pagels emphasizes that Mary Magdalene's great love for, and close relationship with Jesus, was a source of conflict among the disciples:

> The   companion of the (Savior is) Mary Magdalene. (But Christ loved) her more than (all) the disciples and used to kiss her (often) on her (mouth). The rest of (the disciples were offended by it ...).

They said to him, "Why do you love her
more than all of us?" The Savior answered and said to them, "Why do I not
love you as (I love) her?"[19]

Is there a clue in this passage which reveals the later
denigration of Mary Magdalene? Pagels goes on to
describe Peter's anger at Mary Magdalene's account of
Jesus' resurrection. She states that Peter was furious
that the risen Christ had appeared "first to a woman"
and not to his disciples. From the Gnostic accounts in
the *Gospel of Thomas*, the *Gospel of Philip*, and the
Gospel of Mary, it becomes evident that Peter, of all the
disciples, was the most offended by Mary Magdalene's
special relationship with Jesus.

The point must be made that this specific dynamic cannot be overlooked if one gives credence to a
connection between the author of Mark's Gospel and
Peter, in that the author of Mark is writing an account
of Peter's experience. "An unbroken tradition affirms
that the evangelist (i.e. the author of the Gospel of
Mark) was intimately associated with the apostle Peter
and that the contents of this Gospel depend significant-
ly upon the message he proclaimed."[20]

Thus, the canonical book of Mark would be
written to reflect a view sympathetic toward Peter.
One could then conclude that Mary Magdalene's role,
and actual experience with Jesus, has been distorted
(even if this distortion was an unconscious one). Since
historically, many biblical scholars have believed that
Mark was used as the source document for the Gospels
of Matthew and Luke, the definitive body of literature
in the Synoptic Gospels may have, and in all likelihood
did, distort Mary Magdalene's story.[21] The canon, itself,
gives little information about an early schism which

centered around the persons of Mary Magdalene and her detractor, Peter.

However, when Gnostic material is used to fill in the gaps of the accepted canon, a more complete picture emerges, one which reveals the extent of Peter's antagonism toward Mary Magdalene. As an example, in the Gnostic *Gospel of Mary*, Peter says to her, "Sister, we know that the Savior loved you more than the rest of the women. Tell us the words of the Savior which you remember--which you know (but) we do not, nor have we heard them."[22] And Mary Magdalene then tells them she has seen the Lord in a vision. She describes a vision which, in some aspects, is not dissimilar from John's apocalyptic vision recorded in the New Testament book of Revelation.

When she completes her recitation of this vision, both Andrew and Peter discount its authenticity. Andrew remarks, "Say what you (wish to) say about what she has said. I at least do not believe the Savior said this. For certainly these teachings are strange ideas."[23] Then Peter also joins in, angrily saying, "Did he really speak with a woman without our knowledge (and) not openly? Are we to turn about and all listen to her? Did he prefer her to us?"[24]

In these words Peter revealed his wounded ego, and as he projected his anger onto Mary Magdalene she was wounded as well, because the text indicates, "Then Mary wept and said to Peter, 'My brother Peter, what do you think? Do you think that I thought this up myself in my heart, or that I am lying about the Savior?'"[25] Here Levi intervenes, confronting Peter about his anger saying, "Peter, you have always been hot tempered. Now I see you contending against the woman like the adversaries. But if the Savior made her worthy, who are you indeed to reject her? Surely the

Savior knows her very well. That is why he loved her more than us."[26]

When a reader encounters these words, it is not surprising that these sources were declared heretical by those who made the definitive decisions related to the canon. By the time the New Testament canon was set, adherents of the Petrine tradition would have protected Peter at all costs. The man who would become the father of Roman Catholic Christianity was already known for his quick temper and unruly tongue. To add additional emphasis to these character traits would not have served the apologists nor the cause of the early Christian faith.

The Gnostic Gospel reveals the relationship which apparently existed between the human Jesus and Mary Magdalene. This account, and others similar to it, provide subtle clues about her experience at the tomb. Mary Magdalene had stood beneath the cross as Jesus was executed in the bloody, barbaric style of the Romans; he was not executed by a method prescribed by his Hebrew faith. She had stood by him and watched him die; she is the one to whom he appears after he has been raised from the dead.

Elisabeth Schüssler Fiorenza writes, "Thus in a double sense she becomes the *apostola apostolorum*, the apostle of the apostles. She calls Peter and the Beloved Disciple to the empty tomb and she is sent to the 'new family' of Jesus to tell them that Jesus is ascending ... . In contrast to Mark 16:8 we are unambiguously told that Mary Magdalene went to the disciples and announced to them: 'I have seen the Lord.'"[27]

The early distortions of Mary Magdalene's apostolic role have had a powerful impact on her reception in the modern consciousness. But Mary Magdalene is that one who is the first witness to the resurrection.

Even though the gospel of Luke (and the early Christian dogmatics which are evident in I Corinthians 15:3-6) fails to acknowledge her apostolic supremacy, John and Matthew's gospels (as well as the Markan appendix which has been declared "secondary"):

> ... credit primacy of apostolic witness to Mary Magdalene. ... Since the tradition of Mary Magdalene's primacy in apostolic witness challenged the Petrine tradition, it is remarkable that it has survived in two independent streams of Gospel tradition. Moreover, later apocryphal writings ... reflect the theological debate over the apostolic primacy of Mary Magdalene and Peter explicitly.[28]

Unlike Peter, Mary Magdalene had remained loyal to Jesus; she had not denied him three times, nor did she swear (with an oath) that she had not known him. On the contrary, she places herself in a place of jeopardy by going to anoint his body after his death.

The revelation of God, through the resurrection of Jesus, the Christ, is the pivotal key to this controversy. If any divine revelation must be received before it can be regarded as revelatory[29], then the revealed nature of a God who acts to lift Jesus up from death is dependent upon those who witness it. Both the writings of Paul, and those of the Gospel of Mark, center upon God's action in raising Jesus up from the dead as the critical moment of divine revelation in the history of humanity. Those who receive this revelation are then called to witness to it, in order that the revelation be realized in a universal way.[30]

If the revelation of God is through the resurrection, and if the witness to that resurrection is through the apostle who offers its transcendence to the world, then Mary Magdalene, who is the first witness, is the one whom God had chosen for that purpose. This woman would truly be the leader of those who go out to witness. Yet, Mary Magdalene's role was misrepresented by the earliest apologists who wrote the canon and subsequent commentaries on the canon.

Recent English translations of the canon reveal the continuing unconscious protection and elevation of the Petrine tradition. As an example, the translators of the New Revised Standard Version (in explaining the ending of chapter sixteen in Mark) are careful to note that "the most ancient authorities bring the book to a close at the end of Verse 8."[31] By closing the book of Mark with this verse, Mary Magdalene is left dangling on a tether of terror, unable to witness to the resurrection since in Verse 8, "they went out and fled from the tomb, for terror and amazement had seized them; and they said nothing to anyone, for they were afraid."[32] This closure effectively stanches the witness by Mary Magdalene and allows the men who were disciples to claim the hierarchy of power in the early days of Christianity.

Their modern male counterparts unconsciously cling to the same need to claim the keys to the kingdom; the New Revised Standard Version of the Bible was published in 1989 and 1990! But, the contemporary theologian must ask, why did a later scribe include this account which parallels the text from John? Was this scribe trying to elucidate Mary Magdalene's role, in a time when others were already writing to distort it?

Women historians have written of those early patristic fathers whose words have diminished Mary

Magdalene's witness to the resurrection. Caroline Walker Bynum has noted that Aelred of Rievaulx argued:

> She was forbidden to touch him because her faith in the resurrection has wavered. Peter and John go into the tomb, and far from weeping, run away rejoicing. "Only she who did not enter wept, and in her disbelief she thought the body had been carried off deceitfully." It is a woman who did not believe, "for the one who believes, rises to perfect manhood, to the measure of the stature of the fullness of Christ." Her lack of faith is contrasted with that of the faith of the Virgin Mary who had already believed. "When she did not believe, she is woman;" when she begins to be converted, she is called "Mary," that is, she receives the name of her who bore Christ. For a holy soul can be said to bear Christ spiritually.' She is instructed to go to ask "more perfect men" to explain to her the distinction between "my Father and your Father."[33]

This account is one of many which denigrate Mary Magdalene as the first witness to the resurrection, as well as the authenticity and quality of her belief. Instead of allowing Mary Magdalene to be elevated to a level of apostleship based on her transformative experiences with the risen Christ, her story has been related with derogatory overtones. For centuries this projection of the negative onto one woman has been a part of a tradition born by the collective of women.

Historically the threat to male apostleship, and later to the Petrine tradition of male clergy, hangs in the balance and thus these overtones exist. Fiorenza notes:

> The truth of Biblical religion resides in those traditions and texts that are historically reliable, that is, that tell us what actually happened. If for instance, scholars can prove that the "empty tomb stories" in the New Testament are secondary legends of the community, then scholars cannot accord historical reliability and theological significance to the resurrection witness of Mary Magdalene and the women disciples.[34]

So the particular significance of Mary Magdalene's encounter with the risen Christ is diminished, and scholars "claim" that those aspects of the canon which would substantiate her role as the first witness to the resurrection are "secondary" and thus lacking in authenticity.

Yet Mary Magdalene, who had loved Jesus (and had been loved by him) before death, clings tenaciously to her identification as the first person to whom he appears after he has risen. There is a touching poignancy in her recognition of him when he calls her by name; her one word response, "Rabboni," for all its simplicity, reveals a measure of her psychic ties to the human Jesus. One does not use the term *Rabboni* unless one is intimate with the person addressed; otherwise the word *rabbi* would be used. Rabboni is a diminutive, personal usage of the more formal word rabbi.

The splendid numinosity reflected in her vision (related in the Gnostic *Gospel of Mary*) is representative of the profound transformation she experiences when the human Jesus has been raised from death. In her resurrection encounter, Mary Magdalene transcends the limited physicality of her previous relationship with the human Jesus to a new and vital spirituality in relationship with the risen Christ. She learns that she can no longer "touch" him; she cannot "cling" to him.

When Jesus tells Mary Magdalene she can no longer hold on to him, he also tells her, "But go to my brothers and say to them, 'I am ascending to my Father and your Father, to my God and your God.'"[35] In that moment Mary Magdalene learns that she must, herself, "rise up" as an independent woman of faith, as a leader of the early Christian movement. She can no longer deny her own spirituality, her own strength, nor can she project them onto Jesus. He cannot carry her psychic projection of perfect brother, or father, or even lover/-husband. She must stand in the Judean dust and grieve for her companion, for in that grieving will be born the timeless aspects of her leadership of his followers.

Notes

1. Kahlil Gibran, *Spiritual Sayings of Kahlil Gibran*, (Secaucus: The Citadel Press, 1962), 20. Here I have changed Gibran's articulation to an inclusive language form.
2. John McLintock and James Strong, eds., *Encyclopedia of Biblical, Theological and Ecclesiastical Literature* 1873 (Grand Rapids: Baker Book House (1873) reprint 1969), 846.
3. Ibid., 847.

4. Marina Warner, *Alone of All Her Sex, The Myth and The Cult of the Virgin Mary* (New York: Vintage Books, 1976), 229.

5. Elisabeth Moltmann-Wendel, *The Women Around Jesus,* (New York: Crossroad Publishing Co., 1980), 82.

6. Ibid.

7. Ibid.

8. Ibid., 83.

9. M. Warner, *Alone of All Her Sex,* 228.

10. Clinton Morrison, *An Analytical Concordance to the Revised Standard Version of the New Testament,* (Philadelphia: The Westminster Press, 1979), 373.

11. Denise Lardner Carmody, *Biblical Woman, Contemporary Reflections on Scriptural Texts* (New York: Crossroad Publishing Co., 1988), 134.

12. Ronald Brownrigg, *Who's Who in the New Testament* (New York: Crown Publishing Co., 1971), 299.

13. *Diagnostic and Statistical Manual of Mental Disorders,* 3rd ed. -- Revised (Washington, D.C.: American Psychiatric Association, 1987), 217. The emphasis is mine.

14. Brownrigg, *Who's Who,* 300-301.

15. Samuel Fallows, ed., *Bible Encyclopedia and Scriptural Dictionary* (Chicago: Howard Severance Co., 1911), 1122.

16. Edith Deen, *All the Women of the Bible* (San Francisco: Harper & Row Publishers, 1955), 203.

17. Moltmann-Wendel, *The Women Around Jesus,* 69.

18. J. E. Fallon, "St. Mary Magdalene," *New Catholic Encyclopedia,* vol. 9 (New York: McGraw Hill, 1967), 389.

19. Elaine Pagels, *The Gnostic Gospels* (New York: Random House, 1979), 64.

20. William L. Lane, *The Gospel According to Mark*, (Grand Rapids, Mich: Wm. B. Eerdmans Publishing Co., 1974), 7. (The clarification within the parentheses is mine.)

21. Even though New Testament scholar, Werner Kümmel, is skeptical regarding the source (and author) of Mark's Gospel; see Werner Georg Kümmel, *Introduction to the New Testament*, trans. Howard Clark Kee (Nashville, Abingdon Press, 1973), 95-97; one early source, Papias, a bishop in Asia Minor wrote: "Mark, having become the interpreter of Peter, wrote down accurately everything that he remembered, without however recording in order what was either said or done by Christ. For neither did he hear the Lord, nor did he follow Him; but afterwards, as I said, (attended) Peter, who adapted his instructions to the needs (of his hearers) but had no design of giving a connected account of the Lord's oracles." See: Eduard Schweizer's *The Good News According to Mark*, trans. by Donald H. Madvig (Atlanta: John Knox Press, 1970), 25. Schweizer essentially agrees with Kümmel. William L. Lane, however, quotes a number of different sources, who substantiate the theory that Mark's gospel "was the apostolic preaching of Peter." He quotes Iranaeus as writing, "And after the death of these, Mark, the disciple and interpreter of Peter, also transmitted to us in writing the things preached by Peter." See Lane's *The Gospel According to Mark*, 7-12.

22. James Robinson, ed., *The Gospel of Mary, The Nag Hammadi Library in English* (San Francisco: Harper and Row Publishers, 1988), 525.

23. Ibid., 526.

24. Ibid.

25. Ibid.

26. Ibid., 526-27.

27. Elisabeth Schüssler Fiorenza, *In Memory of Her, A Feminist Theological Reconstruction of Christian Origins* (New York: Crossroad Publishing Co., 1985), 332.

28. Ibid.

29. Bishop John Shelby Spong, *Born of a Woman: A Bishop Rethinks The Birth of Jesus* (San Francisco: Harper San Francisco, 1992), 146.

30. Ibid.

31. *The New Revised Standard Version of The Holy Bible* (Nashville: Thomas Nelson, Inc., 1989), 55; also see, *The New Revised Standard Version of the Holy Bible* (Nashville: Cokesbury, 1990), 77.

32. Ibid.

33. Caroline Walker Bynum, quoted in Ann Loades' *Searching for Lost Coins* (Allison Park, PA: Pickwick Publications, 1987), 29.

34. Elisabeth Schüssler Fiorenza, *Bread Not Stone: The Challenge of Feminist Biblical Interpretation* (Boston: Beacon Press, 1984), 11.

35. John 20:17, *The New Revised Standard Version of the Holy Bible* (Nashville: Cokesbury, 1990), 164.

4

The Misogyny of Modern Theology

"Make me, O God, the prey of the lion..."
--Kahlil Gibran, *Sand and Foam*[1]

What would have changed in the Christian tradition had Mary Magdalene's story not been distorted, had she been allowed her status as apostle? Perhaps those male theologians like Schweitzer and Bultmann who (centuries later) struggled to differentiate between the historical human Jesus and the symbolic risen Christ could have seen that Mary Magdalene was the first human to understand this difference. Even as their writing acknowledges that one's reception of that which is sacred or divine is experiential, in that one is always bound by the temporal and cultural context of one's existence, their approach to this problem is a rational, linear one of the mind.

Schweitzer ultimately arrives at a more soul-felt solution than Bultmann, asserting that one cannot "demythologize" that which is essentially symbolic. But Bultmann exhibits the unfortunate tunnel vision of one whose only perspective is unemotional and rational. In dissecting the symbolic and sacred significance of the "Jesus story," Bultmann's methodology never strays from the linear and empirical. The scientific mind does not easily adjust itself to that which is irrational, but the soul and the spirit are at home in this territory.

Mary Magdalene was at home here, as well. She looked into the face of her beloved friend and human companion, and in one soul-searing, numinous moment, she understood that the risen Christ offered a transcendence far exceeding the human encounters of a "historical" Jesus. This is a transformation of ultimate mystery, one which cannot be reduced to mere words, and surely one which is beyond the rigid methodology of empirical theologians and/or scientists.

Mary Magdalene is the first to look into the face of the risen Christ, to encounter the realization of Judaic hope, to spy the future of a glorified God. She is the first to look into the face of one imprinted with the horror of traumatic death and marked by the empowerment of the supreme and divine Holy Spirit.

The experiential aspect of Mary Magdalene's knowledge of the man/god Jesus is vital. Her experience is in keeping with the New Testament understanding of mystery. In this context the Greek word for mystery is *mysterion.* It is defined as experiential knowledge which can only be acquired through a personal and intimate experience. "The word conveys the meaning of an esoteric or mystical knowledge that can be comprehended only by those whose understanding has been enlightened by personal experience with the source and object of its knowing."[2]

Mary Magdalene experienced the resurrected Christ in a palpable way; she then "knew" this raised Jesus at a deeper level than was possible through mind-level reasoning. It was a place of *mysterion.* The inheritance of linear, doctrinal theological predominance has had a profound impact upon women and their spiritual development:

> The Christian faith suffocates within the prison of its patriarchal thought structure. ... The Judeo-Christian religion is tied to a book that was written by men, who thereby introduced the perspective and interests of the dominant male class. Since written theology has until now been able to produce only a distorted and inadequate picture of women and their relationships, we must regard the written tradition of the Judeo-Christian--Old Testament, New Testament, canon law, and dogmatics--as biased and inadequate sources. Matriarchal images or modes of thinking are present only unconsciously or peripherally.[3]

The mysterion, the numinosity of Christian faith, has been drained away by those who insist upon the law, upon its related and stultifying rigidity, and upon a Christianity that is wholly defined by these rational assumptions.

Women have been subtly instructed that their beings are flawed because they understand out of an irrational place, a place of *mysterion.* In their efforts to be accepted into the male-dominated world of the church, and its clergy, many women have unconsciously resorted to emulating men: "The value of written religion has often been overrated. Fascinated by what is for them a newly discovered science, women have often come to regard it as the only source of religion, thereby becoming trapped in male behavior patterns."[4]

Sadly, modern women who seek a meaningful understanding of their God, and strive to enlarge that understanding in a cognitive way, are shackled with the same negative projections and assumptions that hindered Mary Magdalene.   When I read the catalog published by the seminary (where I eventually completed my Master of Divinity degree), out of numerous courses in theology, only one course, labeled "Feminist Theology," was offered to students who would inform themselves using studies completed by women theologians.   This one course stands as a pitiful offering of the work accomplished during the past two decades by theologians who are women.   The title for this class was subtly abrasive because it carried the negative connotations associated with the word feminist.

There was an overwhelming absence of courses which would have exemplified the experience of women.   There were no courses which might have been entitled "The Outstanding Women of the Old and New Testaments," or "Early and Medieval Women Mystics," or "The Women of Judaism," or even "Twentieth Century Women Theologians." However, the percentage of women students, compared to men, belied the applicability for this type of curricula change.   During my years as a student at seminary, fifty percent of the students were women.

Maria Harris, in discussing curricula offered by any institution, indicates that such curricula speaks volumes about the underlying intent of that institution. She uses Eisner's concepts of explicit, implicit, and null curricula to make her point. The explicit curricula offered by my seminary was "what is consciously taught, what is overtly and verbally addressed, what is printed and presented as subject matter to be studied."[5] A required class entitled "Moral Theology," represented the explicit curriculum in a powerful way. While including the works of male theologians (those considered definitive scholars on the dynamics of group process, as it relates to power, authority, and concomitant ethical assumptions), this class did not include even one woman theologian (like Letty Russell) who has written on this subject.

The implicit curriculum is, in contrast, a less tangible presence in the academic arena. It is "found in the interstices and in the atmosphere: patterns of direct address, or of decision making or of designing positions of influence. ... The implicit curriculum refers to 'what really gets said' in what gets said, to 'what really goes on'--subtly and at the margins--in what goes on, in between the lines and in the silences."[6] Here the seminary's admirable struggle with inclusive language was an intriguing example of both a participant and a spectator sport.

I came to seminary with the naive assumption that my denomination was using inclusive language as an indication of its social consciousness, and that inclusive language was assumed to be the norm within any denominational setting. In each class, and in initial orientation sessions, all students were informed that the seminary had taken a specific stance on inclusive language as the only acceptable language for worship liturgy, class instruction, and class discussion. I did not find this surprising, since the denomination had taken

this position a number of years earlier. A measure of
the resistance to this edict was evident when a petition
was circulated by a group of male students, who com-
plained of feeling stifled and unable to participate
because their language of choice was exclusive.

The null curriculum is the most subtle of all in
that "this is a curriculum which exists because it does
not exist, for it refers to ideas left out, ideas not addressed, concepts not offered."[7] The null curricula is
the most insidious of these three categories because, as
Maria Harris notes:

> ... ignorance, not knowing something, is
> never neutral. If we do not know about
> something, or do not realize what is ad-
> dressed can be understood in another
> manner or seen through another lens, it
> skews our viewpoint; it limits our options;
> it clouds our perspective. The thing
> which does not fit in or which is left out
> forcefully educates and miseducates every-
> one, since the thing which is left out or
> forgotten regularly turns out to be the
> clue leading to new knowledge.[8]

While much of the null curricula at seminary had to do
with courses which authentically reflect the experience
and understanding of women, one of the most obvious
aspects of null curricula was evident in the pastoral
care department. Here the approach to counseling was
a cross between the medical, psychiatric model and a
behavioral model. Students were not offered an option
of exploring the concepts of Carl Jung (or Fritz Kunkel) in this area, even though Jung's analytical work has
long been accepted as a viable method of approaching

the psychological wounding of those who seek out (specifically) pastoral care (as opposed to counseling or psychoanalytical therapy in the secular arena).

In 1933 Jung wrote this of his experience with analytical clients:

> Among all my patients in the second half of life--that is to say, over thirty-five-- there has not been one whose problem in the last resort was not that of finding a religious outlook on life. It is safe to say that every one of them fell ill because (they) had lost that which the living religions of every age have given to their followers, and none of them has been really healed who did not regain (this) religious outlook.[9]

Jung was an exception in the psychoanalytical world, one who believed that an experience of the holy was imperative for the healing of soul wounding.

But, standing on their masculine, medical/psychiatric dominated model of teaching, this division of the seminary was overtly hostile to any suggestion that Jungian theory might be feasible or even applicable to the field of pastoral care. Those who held themselves apart, as highly knowledgeable in this field, seemed afraid that their authority was called into question if this theory was, indeed, applied during the course of such learning.

Even so, I suspect that even one semester devoted to an exploration of Jung's work, or that of Fritz Kunkel, would have equipped those students (who were doing clinical training in hostile environments--like prisons) to better understand the underlying psychological dynamics of those who inhabited such settings (as well as their own reactions to such pseudo-clients). Students with little or no previous education in psychology were ill prepared to protect themselves, or their pseudo-clients, in the clinical training process.

The null curricula was evident as a correlation of both the explicit and the implicit curricula in one particular class where a hermeneutical and historical overview of Biblical scripture was presented. While I believe the professor was consciously attempting an incorporation of material which reflected women's scholarship, the end result was to unconsciously sublimate this material into a forgotten realm.

As we progressed through the course material for the semester, the one book written by a woman theologian was set aside for two classes at the end of the semester. This book was ultimately never discussed, its concepts were never incorporated into the lecture material, and though it was addressed in the take-home portion of a final exam, there its applicability was one in which students could critique the book without the challenge of public dialogue.

It must be stated that this book, entitled *God and the Rhetoric of Sexuality*, by Phyllis Trible, was one of the most carefully prepared hermeneutical texts I have studied; to say that it parallels the work of historical (male) hermeneutical methodology is to understate its careful and complete scholarly approach. It exceeded many exegetical or hermeneutical works written by men! Her insights into the original Hebrew language of the Genesis creation myth are superb examples of the scholarly work being done by women theologians. The sadness is that these scholarly works by women fall into the category of null curricula, even as this seminary, in its institutional public relations, talks a different game.

One of the most punitive aspects of my personal spiritual journey came at the hands of males in my judicatory "of care." I was already an ordained elder in my denomination, an ordination that lasts for one's lifetime. But, any person who seeks the office of ordination to become a "Minister of the Word and Sacrament" in the Presbyterian denomination must participate in a two-step candidacy process. This process is a rigorous one, designed to supply churches with clergy who are well-informed, and well-educated, reformed theologians.

The first stage, known as the "inquirer stage," allows candidates to explore their own potential for ministry, as a "called" profession, under the stipulations set by the *Book of Order*, one part of the governing instrument of the denomination. In order to complete the inquirer stage, a candidate must be taken "under care" by a presbytery, whose committee of oversight is known as the "Committee on Preparation."

This committee, like all committees and formal groups who are assigned tasks within the denomination, is to be composed of members representative of the gender-related percentages within that governing body. Despite the percentage of women members in my former presbytery, (percentages that exceeded fifty percent), my committee was composed of five men and two women, one of whom was a clergywoman and (later) the chair of the committee.

The gender composition of this committee should have been the first red flag for me, but I was disproportionately trusting of those who were to care for me. I had worked as the staff financial officer of this presbytery for six years before I departed for seminary. I loved the people in this presbytery; they had affirmed me in the work I had done on their staff, and I had no reason to suspect that my new initiative would be viewed in any way except positively. And on a purely rational level, I suspect that those men who served on this committee would claim that they had, indeed, cared for me as I went through this process. But, on a visceral, archetypal level they revealed some startling and ugly psychic material during my candidacy. Their projections onto me were so unexpected, and so unconsciously demeaning, that I came away from every meeting psychically reeling.

To say those three years under care were unpleasant would be to put a pretty face on them. To say they were more punitive than they needed to be, they had a powerfully negative impact upon my soul, and they were remarkably lacking in Christian compassion would be an accurate assessment of them. The words of the clergywoman who spoke of a "broken spirit" (when she bade me farewell as I left North Dakota for seminary) echoed in my mind often during those three years. My spirit was not broken by what occurred at seminary, but it was surely bruised and battered by those who were responsible for my care process at the presbytery level.

My first clue to the ensuing ugliness came the first time I had lunch with the committee after a formal meeting (to review the progress I had made during my first year at the seminary). One of the men (a "professional" man who was then retired and in his late sixties or early seventies) began that meal by telling an off-color joke which was blatantly sexual and derogatory toward women. This unprofessional demeanor might have been overlooked had it occurred only once, but the following year, in the same setting, he told another, equally offensive joke. When this happened for the second time, I determined that I would not again put myself in this vulnerable place, where I would be forced to hear one of his jokes, and thus I refused to eat another meal with this group.

I believe the journey toward ordination is littered with charred bones of candidates who have been seared by the projectory fires of their caretakers. (Most of these charred bones belong to women.) I came close to being one of those who lie in the ditch between intentionality and realized actuality. In the first stages of this process, there were subtle hints that colored the environment of my conversations with this committee. But, I had the qualifications for what would ordinarily be considered a strong candidate. I had completed the requirements for my undergraduate degree in two years.[10] In reaction to this I was told, by the committee, that I would *not* be permitted to graduate early from seminary, that I must take the usual three years to complete this second degree. That rationale might have been a reasonable one had I been age twenty, but I was forty-seven years old when I entered seminary. One of my very real concerns was age discrimination when I sought a position after seminary.

Not unlike many other seminary students, I had life changes during these years that had a dramatic impact upon my psychic and physical health. Three days after I arrived on the campus, I received a call from a dermatologist who had removed a suspicious looking mole from just above the elbow on the inside of my right arm. He indicated that the mole had been a malignant melanoma; the tissue must be surgically excised to prevent a further life-threatening spread of this melanoma. Several weeks later I had out-patient surgery; the surgeon removed approximately half of my right bicep. Three weeks later the fall schedule of classes began. Since I am right handed, my writing arm was seriously disabled for the first several months of that semester.

During this same period of time my mother, who had been ailing for more than a year, stumbled toward her dying with intermittent stays in the hospital. Whenever I could get away, I would drive the eight-hour trip to Virginia to see her. Ultimately, she spent the month of January in the hospital and I drove back and forth during this time, coming back to seminary to manage my work there, and then driving back to sit with my sister as we watched over my mother during her last days. When she died in February, it was the second trauma during my first six months at the seminary.

The committee charged with my care sent no letters indicating their awareness that I had been traveling this tumultuous journey. I received no affirming phone calls, no "get-well" cards during or after the surgery, no notes of condolence when my mother died, nothing. I *was* told, when I met with the committee in April, two months after my mother's death, that they were concerned because I appeared to be "disengaged." They noted that I seemed to have no local (seminary related) church affiliation, and I had not "done any field work yet"! All this came with no acknowledgement of a necessary grieving time; there was literally no pastoral care offered to me by this committee. Their criticism was reiterated the following year, after I had completed a clinical training program in a local hospital. But, the underlying critique, the subtle undertone throughout the course of my care process, was one of unconscious, and yet deliberate, rejection of my abilities and my continuing work because I was a woman.

There is no other way the attitude of the committee can be interpreted, since I never missed a course deadline, even when my mother lingered on the abyss of dying. I had received superior evaluations for the work I was required to do throughout the three years at seminary. But, even so, the committee continued to treat me as if I were a sub-standard student, who surely was not suitable material for the ministry!

In my second year the committee decided I had problems with "conflict management" and issued an edict requiring me to work with someone who could instruct me in such matters. I was also told I had a problem with "authority issues." Well, they were right there! I surely have problems with a blatant abuse of authority, which this committee exemplified. Nevertheless, over the next year I spent more than two thousand additional dollars in order to honor their stringent requirements. Essentially what I was required to do involved paying for my own pastoral care!

In my senior year, along with other graduating seniors, I was instructed (by seminary staff) that my resumé should be prepared and ready for release by the end of November, or at the latest by the middle of December. The seminary placement office works overtime to assist graduating students in locating positions; their office begins this work in November and continues it until the student graduates. But, when I sent my completed resumé to the committee (after having it reviewed, and approved, by the Dean of Students), they refused to release it until they had their "regular" meeting at the end of January. Again, the committee was showing me, in a tangible way, the power they held over my future. I did not receive the committee's approval until the first week in February, two months after the seminary deadline (and two months after I had sent the resumé to them).

My final interview with this committee echoes in

my mind like a verbal *Clockwork Orange* nightmare. While candidates are urged to speak their conscience, the unwritten rules of the game demand that one "play the game." By playing the game where the rules are determined by patristic patterns and old traditional assumptions, many women find their integrity is sacrificed in order to achieve the ultimate goal: ordination. Nevertheless, the Presbyterian Church, U.S.A. declares, "that 'God alone is the Lord of the conscience, and hath left it free from the doctrines and commandments of men, which are in anything contrary to his Word, or beside it, in matters of faith or worship.'"[11] Thus, any question asked of a candidate has a subjective quality, since the response must ultimately be one of individual conscience. As I made my way through the verbal gauntlet that was my "exit interview," I knew intuitively that (those who opposed me on) the committee were going to vote against declaring me "ready for ordination," no matter what I said. The questions were ones which demanded that I declare the Bible to be inerrant, even though reasonably informed, well-educated theologians cannot possibly hold to such a stance.

Many outsiders believe the Presbyterian Church U.S.A. is a denomination whose clergy would rarely be categorized as "fundamentalists." The denomination, itself, has historically demanded that its clergy be well-educated, and liberal theologians have been part of the visible face of the Presbyterian Church over the years. The requirement for studying Hebrew and Greek is held up as part of the high standards set by this denomination. However, in the past ten to fifteen years, there has been a backlash of conservative and ultra-conservative thinking within my denomination. Those who are part of this backlash were strongly represented on my care committee. They are:

> those whose religious security is rooted in a literal Bible (and who) do not want that security disturbed. They are not happy when facts challenge their biblical understanding or when nuances in the text are introduced or when they are forced to deal with either contradictions or changing insights. The Bible, as they understand it, shares the permanence and certainty of God, convinces them that they are right, and justifies the enormous fear and even negativity that lie so close in fundamentalistic religion. For biblical literalists, there is always an enemy to be defeated in mortal combat.[12]

In the eyes of those who opposed me on this committee, I had become the target for such projections; I had been translated into "the enemy." They made this projection abundantly clear as the questions continued, and my answers were dissected, misconstrued, and reinterpreted from their fundamentalistic perspective. The negative projection was so apparent in the end that my energy was thoroughly sapped; I could feel the natural energy I usually carry being drained away, as if someone had slit my psychic wrists.

Finally, all the grief and rage that I had carried throughout this tortuous process rolled up into my throat, and I thought to myself, "If you're going to take me out anyway, you will not do so because I have lied to appease you. So, I will not lie, I will at least go down speaking honestly from my authentic belief." In reaction to my answers, several members of the committee filed a minority report when this committee report came to the floor of the presbytery.

They would have blocked my ordination had it not been for my friends in that presbytery, who stood to my defense and refused to allow the minority report to sway the vote in a negative way. And so, after this trial by fire, I was approved for ordination by my presbytery of care. The vote of the committee had been very, very close; I do not have the data on the presbytery vote.

Then (like all other candidates) I had to face oral examinations by the Committee on Preparation of the presbytery where the church which called me is located. After that, like all other candidates, I was "examined on the floor" of the ordaining presbytery. Probably the most heartening comment in this final stage of the process came at the end of this last oral examination. As I was escorted from the sanctuary by the Stated Clerk of the presbytery, he looked at me with a grand smile lighting his face and exclaimed, "You have just 'conducted' the finest ordination exam I have ever heard on the floor of this presbytery!" And then, the fiery trials ended, with a unanimous vote by a presbytery of folks who were strangers.

I am not naive enough to believe my experience is an isolated, unique one. Women who enter the ministry today still bear the brunt of subtle, covert misogyny. While the mistreatment may be less apparent, because it is carefully cloaked in denominational double-speak, it mirrors the abusive, defamatory tones of one like Martin Luther, who said of Mary Magdalene, "She loved him (Jesus) with a hearty, lusting, rutting love"; she had a "hot, lusting, rutting heart for him."[13]

Here Luther takes what may (or may not) have been a sexual relationship between Jesus and Mary Magdalene and projects his own worst psychic, shadow material onto her womanhood, in a way that leaves her seeming like the wanton whore many Christians believe her to be. His words are unequivocal in the image they portray, and that image is an ugly one. The projection of Luther's own psychic material must be emphasized here; it is the kind of projection that continues even today. The elderly man on my committee, who consistently told off-color sexist jokes, revealed the same kind of unconscious psychological material in those jokes. His inability to view women as professional colleagues, and worthy of a concomitant respect, is rooted in the archetypal evil of his own shadow.

But worse than the snide innuendo of his jokes was the attitude of the clergyman who seemed determined to stop my ordination, at almost any cost. This pastor spearheaded the movement to bring the minority report to the floor of presbytery and did his utmost to deprive me of ordination. Throughout my care process, this pastor was overtly hostile toward me, and his body language reflected his unconscious, negative projection onto me.

At one meeting he sat directly across from me in a circle of chairs. Throughout the time that I conversed with the committee, he sat with his legs spread widely apart, bouncing his lower torso in a manner that was obvious and offensive. While his words carefully cloaked the hatred he (apparently) felt, his body revealed the extent of his nonverbal meaning. The hatred he chose to project onto me needed to be withdrawn and addressed in a therapeutic setting, where an analyst could have confronted him about his negative mother complex.[14]

When the institutional church sets forth its understandings of the journey toward ordination for the ministry of the "Word and Sacrament," that journey should be one of sacred, nurturing containment. When this process is contaminated by strangling patriarchal pronouncements and projections, it loses the radiance of discovered mysterion. It then degenerates into an unconscious, bloody crucifixion, demanding that the lamb be slaughtered but (equally unconsciously) failing to honor the sacrifice. The care/candidacy process in the Presbyterian Church U.S.A. mirrors the dysfunctional characteristics of a denomination struggling to protect the very institution of itself. Like many dysfunctional family units, it elevates a father who has lost his potential to transform, while asking the mother to acquiesce in this inauthentic elevation. The care process could be so much more, so soul-enriching, so heart-uplifting, and yet, it is not.

The journey we share as humans of two genders, each of which has its own particularity and richness, is one that could be enhanced enormously in this care process. It could be one which understands that we are, none of us, complete unto ourselves. We are only complete in relationship with each other and with God. "All human persons stand in solidarity before God. But on the other hand, humankind is a community, male and female. And none is the full image of God alone. Only in the community of humankind is God reflected. God is, according to this bold affirmation, not mirrored as an individual but as a community."[15] If we cut off relationship with others, of either gender, we cut ourselves off from the necessary mirroring which enables us to find a balanced image of God. It is this balanced image of God which is missing from the collective Christian imagination.

Like many other women who have entered the ranks of the clergy, I have paid a price. I paid the actual dollars that two degrees cost, but I paid much more in the psychic and physical tears of blood that were extracted during my journey under care. To be a "candidate under care" is to know the meaning of ultimate powerlessness. In the Presbyterian Church, U.S.A., the oversight committee holds one's life, and one's whole future career, in their hands. Whether those hands are competent is a vital question. If those who sit on these committees are *not* persons of integrity, and honor, who are capable of thinking which reflects social consciousness, the candidate will fare poorly in the process.

A conscious awareness on the part of the oversight committee of the elements of Joseph Campbell's "hero's journey" would have lent more credibility to the way my own care process was conducted. If the committee, the presbytery, and the church itself, openly acknowledged this psychic death/rebirth motif, the student (of either gender, and thus either a "heroine" or a "hero") would be honored in a more soul-caring way.

The ordination process within my denomination is not labeled an initiation. Its proponents are not that honest; nor are they conscious enough to lead an initiation that is wholistic and soul enhancing. An initiation which centers upon the perceived and projected weaknesses of the initiate, while refusing to affirm the strengths, is a part of the one-sided propensity for value judgments that was implicit in my care process. Initiation, as such, can be transforming. But, when the initiators are incapable of owning its reality, the initiation degenerates into torture.

The seminary, through its orientations, and through the honesty of its individual faculty members, was much more aware of this than the institutional church. I remember one professor who used the analogy of Marine boot camp to describe the seminary experience. The Marine Corps' philosophy is one of breaking the ego to bring young soldiers into compliant obedience to their superior officers' orders. For the church to unconsciously emulate this pattern is a sad commentary upon its understandings of preparation for the ministry. Ministry that begins from brokenness can be powerful, but for the candidate to be pushed from a place of psychic health to brokenness is destructive.

The church (from what seems to be a purely unconscious place) emulates another pattern of initiation which is far more applicable, and far more understandable, except that the church, itself, does/can not acknowledge this, because it is derived from the primordial memory of the psyche. The mystery cults of the Greco-Roman world, from whom the concept of the mysterion is derived, flourished from the seventh century B.C.E. to the fourth century C.E. Theirs was an acknowledged process of initiation.

These cults had four distinctive characteristics, ones which were very much an unconscious part of the care process I endured. First, in the mystery cults, the "candidate" for initiation was put through some exercise which caused them to share in the fate of the god. My conversations with the committee, particularly my exit interview, were an unconscious parallel of the unjust aspects of Jesus' hearings before he was condemned to death. Second, those who wished to become a part of the cult must undergo some kind of initiation; "the uninitiated are denied both access to the sacred actions and knowledge of them." Few candidates ever reveal to their congregations, or even to their best friend, the initiation aspects of the candidacy process.

My initiation was comprised of additional (and financially) burdensome requirements which were a manifestation of the committee's need to declare its control and authority over me. Third, salvation is promised to their devotees by the gods who are the cultic heads and with whom the initiates seek union. While every profession has its requirements, a profession whose members declare themselves to be "called by God" has salvation and union with that God as its core reality. Finally, "in all the mysteries the distinction between initiates and non-initiates finds expression not only in the ritual of the celebrations but also in the vow of silence laid on devotees. This is essential to all the mysteries, and is a feature implicit in the etymology."[16]

In my belief this "implicit" vow of silence, related to the punitive aspects of the care process, itself, has been the most devastating part of its hold on those who have experienced a hurtful, wounding process. There are any number of candidates who pass through the ordination process and do not find it to be a negative experience. I submit that most of these are male. But, those who are psychically injured by it, primarily women, know intuitively that their woundedness is not honored by the church hierarchy. They know to maintain this unconsciously, implicitly mandated vow of silence. For, if they don't, their careers within the denomination will suffer.

The institutional church too often takes its women candidates and (in the words of D. H. Lawrence) their souls are "sponged out, erased, dipped into oblivion." Campbell's mythological hero is granted a rebirth at the end of the ego dying journey, a rebirth of transcendent proportions, a rebirth that illuminates the very reason for the previous suffering.

The mythological rebirth is rarely granted within the institutional church because the church has historically denied these primordial aspects of the candidacy initiation. My own spiritual rebirth did not come until I was lovingly received into the collective arms of a congregation in a small rural church. And God bless them for their warm, loving reception of me! But, the "bloody journey from Sumer" continues, because the covert and overt misogyny continues. To my mind, the covert misogyny, with its insidious, sadistic characteristics, is more damaging because the person to whom it is directed may be in a powerless position (i.e. a candidate under care), and thus unable to respond in a self-protective manner.

This misogynistic environment feeds the anger that so many women have held within their bodies/-souls for generations. Women who carry such anger are often berated for their attitudes by those (males and their female peers) who have no understanding of the depth of grief which feeds the anger. It may seem surprising that women clergy would chide their peers for such anger. But, these women, themselves, have denied their own anger for so long they have ceased to believe it occurred in the first place. It has been sublimated and pushed down into the body/psyche and they prefer not to have it remembered. Its memory will burst forth when they are confronted with the same emotion from a peer.

Christopher Durang has written of anger: "Unless you go through all the genuine angers you feel, both justified and unjustified, the feelings of love that you do have will not have any legitimate base and will be at least partially false. Plus, eventually you will go crazy."[17] There are many women in the ranks of today's clergy who dance dangerously close to this "crazy" edge. Their anger is an authentic part of the grief that has been triggered by their treatment in the institutional church, but that anger has not been allowed its voice. It is stifled, ignored, or discounted as the predictable temperament of "one of those feminists." When this occurs the anger is held in the body, only to emerge in gained or lost weight, or in a somatic illness, sometimes in the fatal form of cancer. In fact, the anger can be a killing thing; it eats away at the interiority. It slams up against the walls of church assumptions erected on foundations of dogmatic rigidity. By having it denied, it is unconsciously pushed into a place of devouring an already wounded soul.

One of the apparent criteria used to deny this anger is a determination of whether or not it is justified. Arthur Frank points out, however, "The only reason to sort out angers as justified or not is to make moral judgments on the validity of those angers, to weigh fault and to assess blame ..."[18] Healing can only come about when the anger of countless women is articulated in an arena which demands the attention of the institutional church. Yet, more often, the church responds in ways that are accusatory and demeaning for the one who is angry.

One of the palpable frustrations of my care process was the lack of acknowledgement of my "justified" anger. When I expressed it, the betrayal was compounded by those who claimed that my anger was unjustified, and that I "should have played by the rules of the game." The rules of the game, it must be noted, were male assumptions of a "norm" that force women to accede to that norm, and in the doing of it, to relinquish both their intellectual and soul integrity. When their integrity and authenticity have been sacrificed on the journey toward ordination, women clergy carry this wounding with them into their individual parishes, where it may linger for years, never to be healed.

I recall a brief conversation that occurred when the committee members of my oversight committee had filed out of the room after my final interview. I was angry--and more than angry; I felt stunned and deeply betrayed. I was then asked by the one individual who remained in the room why I could not apply the concepts from my own "Statement of Faith." (See Appendix B) Why could I not honor that God-imprinted image within those who had treated me badly? I sat in shock and disbelief; it was the equivalent of asking why I could not *be* Jesus in that moment.

I was (and am) incapable of that kind of suprahuman feeling. I was angry, and that anger (as a valid reaction) was not only denied, it was treated in the way the church has treated anger for centuries. This person tried to make me feel guilty because I was angry. An attempt to extract a guilty response for anger will neither assuage its reality nor foster its healing.

The notion that anger is an emotion that will fade with time is simplistic and gives no credence to the powerful energies that are triggered by and through the initial eruption of the anger. Women clergy are angry because their souls have been summarily dismissed by a dogmatic, creedal tradition that perceives any questioning of itself as deviant. That unconscious labeling of a genuine emotion continues the tradition of a social institution that has failed to address the depths of its misogyny, even as it denies the feeling components that are a powerful part of a reaction to that misogyny.

Numerous examples of misogynistic statements by the earliest Christian theologians have been recorded. Among them Tertullian is quoted as writing regarding Gnostic Christian women: "These heretical women--how audacious they are! They have no modesty; they are bold enough to teach, to engage in argument, to enact exorcisms, to undertake cures, and it may be, even to baptize![19] Here Tertullian is exhibiting the characteristic outrage of early male clergy at women who dared overstep societal boundaries regarding their "proper" roles.

Tertullian's words are remarkably applicable to the experience of women clergy in the contemporary institution of the church. These words are no longer uttered aloud by the hierarchy, they are unconsciously carried within and projected outward in the same unconscious way. Tertullian was more honest, more forthright, even as he went on to fume: "It is not permitted for a woman to speak in church, nor is it permitted for her to teach, nor to baptize, nor to offer (the eucharist), nor to claim for herself a share in any masculine function--not to mention any priestly office."[20]

If this particular pronouncement sounds familiar; it is because a similar passage can be found in the pseudo-Pauline book of I Timothy 2:11-14. Another comprises part of Paul's instructions to the church at Corinth (I Corinthians 14:33-35). Paul, like Tertullian, was ego-maniacal enough to believe that he was capable of defining what was "Truth."

A definitive aspect of this unconscious, early outrage had to do with Jesus' disregard for orthodox Jewish tradition in his interactions with women. Jesus did not honor the old laws of Judaism in the ways he lived with and treated women. For many women theologians Jesus then becomes "liberator," both for women and for oppressed peoples of the world. This is the primary motif found in "liberation theology," a theology whose beleaguered understanding of an enfleshed God is attacked at every angle by traditionalists who would protect the hierarchical institution of the church.

Jesus' stance cast him into the place of one who was charged with sedition, who was the ultimate "traitor." Jesus, in failing to protect the patriarchy was:

... thus a traitor to the old dispensation, the established collective container of religious values. This explains Caiaphas' attitude when he says in John 11:50, "It is expedient for us, that one man should die for the people, and that the whole nation perish not." The expressed fear of the priests was that, "If we let him thus alone, all men will believe on him, and the Romans shall come and take away both our place and our nation." (John 11:48) But even without the Romans, Christ threatens Jewish orthodoxy. He is therefore on trial for heresy. For a religious community heresy is spiritual treason, more dangerous than treason to the state. We can measure the degree of psychic threat by the intensity of the defensive reaction evoked.[21]

Both the orthodox Jews of Jesus' time and later Christian "fathers of the church" have difficulty with Jesus' attitude toward women. Their modern counterparts, mirroring a literal translationist viewpoint, would protect the "purity" of the clergy and the church. Those who would keep women from places of leadership within the church continually reveal "the degree of their psychic threat, by the (very) intensity of their defensive reaction."

One of the more recent examples of the libidinal energy expressed, and acted out, against women who seek a recognized place as clergy came when the Church of England voted on November 11, 1992, approving women to the priesthood. With this vote of approval came cries of denunciation from leaders of this particular branch of the Christian church, along with shouts of jubilation from the women who had anxiously awaited the (ultimately close) vote. George Carey, the Archbishop of Canterbury, said following that vote:

> We are not departing from a traditional concept of ministry. We are talking about an extension of the same ministry to include women. ...
> Some will argue that we have no right to make changes on our own. We know that the Roman Catholic Church and the Orthodox Churches do not at present countenance this change. That, however, cannot be an obstacle to the Church of England determining its own mind. Article 20 makes clear that the Church of England--I quote-- 'hath authority in controversies of faith.'
> I am well aware that there are those who are profoundly troubled by the ecumenical implications of a yes vote today. ... Significant parts of Christendom do not ordain women to the priesthood, but there are many traditions in which the experience of women in ministry is not a burden, but a joy, not a handicap to mission, but a strength. We must not look in one direction only. ... [22]

There is a subtle quality of apology, and a ponderous attempt at explanation, interwoven throughout this statement by the Archbishop of Canterbury. Specifically, there is an abrasive dichotomy set up by using

opposite words like "burden" and "handicap" to off-set
ones like "joy" and "strength." It leads one to wonder if,
the Archbishop, himself, is one of those who was "profoundly troubled" by this affirmative vote. The usage of
the word "countenance," regarding those hierarchical
churches which still prohibit women clergy, suggests all
the unconscious baggage derived from authoritarian
institutional structures with legalistic ways of issuing
edicts to those they have declared to be inferior. That
the ordaining of women clergy in 1992 should remain a
"controversy of the faith" is a terrible example of the
ongoing *habits of the mind* which hamper human efforts
at wholistic and authentic living of personal spirituality.
It is a sad commentary on a social institution that
claims to be "Christian."

But "the intensity of the defensive reaction
evoked" speaks to underlying psycho-social mores of the
culture. All cultures and societies hold certain practices
or behaviors to be the norm; any departure from the
norm is regarded as anomic or deviant. Here Veblen's
theory is applicable because an underlying psychological
dynamic undergirds the societal structure, one of *habits
of the mind*. These *habits of the mind* are driven by
powerful unconscious imperatives which provide the
stultifying influence for repression of social change.
The norms assumed by the Judeo-Christian tradition
have formed our *habits of the mind*.

The Judaic culture was decidedly and unequivo-
cally patriarchal. Its patriarchy was no accident, but
had gleaned its strength in adverse reaction to the
goddess-worshiping cultures of the Near East. For
Jesus, a proclaimed Son of God, to treat women in an
egalitarian way was truly a threat to the established
order of that time and place.

Thus, the Judaic culture of the day exhibited

typical *habits of the mind* in protecting its cultural norms. Out of the Judaic tradition of accepted and acknowledged patriarchy, a new religion evolved, Christianity. This new religion, in defining its own standards, created norms for those who espoused this new faith that were, essentially, tainted. They were tainted with the Judaic and cultural assumption of male superiority. But, the males who had been the followers of Jesus before his death exhibited little courage and/or superiority in the face of that death.

When Jesus was crucified, in the ensuing turmoil as his followers struggled to define themselves as Christians, one woman, Mary Magdalene, stood out as a leader.[23] She and the other women who were Jesus' companions on his human journey were bold enough to remain the visible supporters of a man who had been labeled a "traitor." With this woman and her sisters the Christ movement began; they were the ones who risked Roman justice when, taking their spices, they went to the tomb to anoint the crucified body of Jesus.

But those to whom the leadership of this early movement has been attributed are men; the history and experience of early women leaders was lost to later generations of Christians. These same men then unconsciously reached deeply into their psychological comfort zones and began to set the limitations and norms by which Christians would live. They began to write the Biblical texts to form a book which became known as accepted canon, as the "Word of God." And their unconscious gave them back an accepted pattern, a *habit of the mind* of male dominance, which was then protected as the norm, but *also* as the accepted Word of God.

This Word of God presented males as the acknowledged leaders, since the misogynistic "polemics of the patristic authors against women's ecclesial leadership and office ultimately resulted in the equation of women's leadership in the church with heresy."[24] Women, who would learn of the color and texture and fiber of this time--and who would enlarge their vision of God beyond those limited parameters, must look beyond the canon to works that have been historically declared heretical.

Women today inherit this unconscious *habit of the mind*--Word of God tradition, even as Mary Magdalene's role was misrepresented by numerous male theologians who sought to protect the norm. The critical point here (and one which must not be overlooked) is that this process occurs "without rational reflection." It is perceived as normal, so that any divergence from it is regarded as anomic and/or deviant.

Another critical aspect of Veblen's theory (and the reason it is so remarkably applicable to this study) is the norms' "resistance to change." When many role expectations for women are considered, society tends to fall back on that source which is regarded as the Truth: the Bible. Even though "the material conditions that gave rise" to the Biblical text "have disappeared," the cultural assumptions of the Bible, as Truth, lead even informed, reasonably intelligent leaders of the current time to push women into stereotypical Biblical models. The insidious nature of a continued patriarchal pattern is not what is evident (so much) on the surface, but the psychological assumptions which underlie the surface actuality.

Notes

1. Kahlil Gibran, *Sand and Foam* (New York: Alfred A Knopf, 1981), 8.
2. John Sanford, *Healing Body and Soul: The Meaning of Illness in the New Testament and in Psychotherapy* (Louisville, Westminster/John Knox Press, 1992), 125.
3. Elisabeth Moltmann-Wendel with Jürgen Moltmann, *Humanity in God* (New York: The Pilgrim Press, 1983), 40 & 41.
4. Ibid.
5. Maria Harris, *Women and Teaching* (New York: Paulist Press, 1988), 19.
6. Ibid., 20.
7. Ibid.
8. Ibid., 20-21.
9. Carl G. Jung, *Modern Man In Search of a Soul*, 229. Here I have changed Jung's articulation to an inclusive language form.
10. Nevertheless, I was an honor graduate (summa cum laude--Phi Beta Kappa), one who would usually be considered favorably for graduate level work.
11. See the "Westminster Confession of Faith," 6.109-2., and the 1991-92 *Book of Order* G-1.0301, Presbyterian Church U.S.A., published by the Office of the General Assembly, 100 Witherspoon St., Louisville, KY.
12. Bishop John Shelby Spong, *Rescuing the Bible from Fundamentalism: A Bishop Rethinks the Meaning of Scripture* (San Francisco: Harper San Francisco, 1991), 3. I have added the words within the parentheses.
13. Martin Luther quoted by Elisabeth Moltmann-Wendel, *Humanity in God*, 14.

14. I have been "diagnostic" in labeling this complex. The complex is an internalized concretization of archetypal material and carries powerful libidinal energy. My own experience in Jungian analysis has taught me much about my own complexes and archetypes, and it was invaluable as I made my way through the shadow projections that were part of study for the ministry. It has also heightened my awareness of the unconscious motivations and complexes of others. I was older than this "pastor," and his projection onto me had more to do with his own (apparent) experience with his birth mother, than it did with the reality of my relationship to him.

15. Walter Brueggemann, *Genesis* (Atlanta: John Knox Press, 1982), 34.

16. Gerhard Kittel, ed., and Geoffrey W. Bromley, trans. and ed., *Theological Dictionary of the New Testament*, vol 4 (Grand Rapids, Mich.: Wm. B. Eerdmans Publishing Co., 1965), 803-806.

17. Christopher Durang, quoted in Arthur W. Frank's "Anger, Illness, and Healing," *Second Opinion*, 17, No 4 (April, 1992): 11.

18. Ibid., p. 13.

19. Tertullian quoted in E. Pagel's *The Gnostic Gospels* (New York: Random House, 1979), 60.

20. Ibid.

21. Edward F. Edinger, *The Christian Archetype, A Jungian Commentary on the Life of Christ* (Toronto: Inner City Books, 1987), 85-86.

22. George Carey, Archbishop of Canterbury, quoted in "Announcements," a news article in *Monday Morning: A Magazine for Presbyterian Leaders*, 58, No 1, (January 11, 1993), 23.

23. Elisabeth Meier Tetlow, *Women and Ministry in the New Testament* (Lanham: University Press of America, Inc., 1980), 118.

24. Elisabeth Schüssler Fiorenza, *In Memory Of Her, A Feminist Theological Reconstruction of Christian Origins* (New York: Crossroad Publishing Co., 1985), 54.

5

Rushing Toward Body Denial

"These plants that live upon the tree draw the milk of the earth in the sweet stillness of night, and the earth in her tranquil dreaming sucks at the breast of the sun."
--Kahlil Gibran, *The Garden of the Prophet*[1]

Early in its history, Christian fathers of theology struggled to define the tenets of the faith regarding chastity, virginity, sexuality, and all that was implied by (a separation of) "the flesh and the Spirit." The impact of Christianity, with its stipulated norms, was great in that it defined women and women's roles in the same restrictive ways as earlier Levitical law. Although their Judaic predecessors had almost completed the annihilation of Near Eastern goddess-worship, elements of its rituals were incorporated into the ritual of the Christian Church (just as these rituals had been adopted earlier into Jewish ritual).

As an example, the ritual of baptism, while its origins were believed to be "transformed" in the baptism of Jesus in the Jordan, was the inherited ritual of the Jewish *mikvah*, the bath of purification. The *mikvah*, as a cleansing bath, is observed even in today's culture as symbolic of contrasting norms for the genders. Lis Harris' quote from a conversation with a woman who is Hasidic is telling when this woman declares, "I feel like a new bride each month, ... How many married women can say that?"[2] Here is an extraordinary acknowledgement of the syncretized imagery of earlier goddess ritual, in that those women who served the goddess as sacred priestesses regularly went to bathe in "sacred springs" which were believed to be hymen renewing, thus allowing them to remain perpetual "virgins."[3]

But the sacred quality of the sexual rituals of this earlier polytheistic tradition was distorted, first by the Levitical pronouncements of Jewish priests who determined that males must have a defined superior role, and later by the men who set the parameters for Christianity. Merlin Stone, in her book entitled *When God Was a Woman*, writes about the sacred temple *qadishtu*, the women who served the goddess by engaging in sexual intercourse. She writes:

> Women who made love in the temples were known in their own language as "sacred women," "the undefiled." Their Akkadian name of *qadishtu* is literally translated as "sanctified women" or "holy women." Yet the sexual customs in even the most academic studies of the past two centuries were nearly always described as "prostitution," the sacred women repeat-

edly referred to as "temple prostitutes" or "ritual prostitutes." The use of the word "prostitute" as a translation for *qadishtu* not only negates the sanctity of that which was held sacred, but suggests, by the inferences and social implications of the word, an ethnocentric subjectivity on the part of the writer. It leads the reader to a misinterpretation of the religious beliefs and social structures of the period.[4]

The sacred aspect of sexual intercourse, and of "holy women," was lost for succeeding generations as the Hebrews and their Christian successors sought to establish cultures in opposition to the practices of the earlier goddess-worshipers. Even today, as Hasidic Judaism prescribes strict stipulations for sexual intercourse between married persons, Talmudic edicts about the impurity of women distort the quality of the very thing which is supposedly deemed sacred to strict orthodoxy, i.e. sexual intercourse.

Early Christian theologians also exhibited an almost obsessive attitude about sexuality issues, an obsession which at times reflected the cultural norms of the Greco-Roman world in which they lived, and at others seemed to take on a decidedly psychotic tone. All the great fathers of the church made profound proclamations which mirrored both their societal expectations and their own personal psychological demons. One noted theologian of the day, Clement of Alexandria, observed that "pagan sexual morality aimed merely at the control of sexual desire, whereas Christian teaching advocated the extirpation of desire itself."[5]

Here Clement demonstrates the influence of Greco-Roman thought upon Christianity, in that both of these cultures, in developing sophisticated thought about sexual intercourse, moved to a stance which was, at its core, decidedly ascetic. The ascetic model can neither perceive normal human sexuality as a gift from God, nor that it could be declared "good" by a creator God. Typical of these prevailing [ascetic] attitudes was the statement of Soranus, "Men who remain chaste are stronger and better than others and pass their lives in better health."[6]

Thus a tone is set; with a denial of sexuality as healthy, a firm and unequivocal separation between the body and the spirit is handed down. Along with this, women are pushed further into an inferior sensual mold. The Mary Magdalene projection is amplified, diversified, and calcified. The value system which evolves holds great significance in that: "The worship of a divinity as male or female expresses an existential value system and a mode of perception in which one archetypal gender prevails over the other in psychological relevance, *being as convincing and determinative for women* as it is for men."[7]

God is male, thus males are superior. What hope do women have, unless they deny the very essence of themselves, their authentic femaleness and seek to become like men? The woman who would achieve some semblance of this masculine superiority would deny her own tendency to completeness (through feminine being) by attempting a perfection achieved through masculine doing.

This undertone of women becoming like men in order to be worthy of note in Christian circles is evident in the Gnostic *Gospel of Thomas*:

> Simon Peter said to them, "Let Mary leave us, for women are not worthy of

life." Jesus said, "I myself shall lead her in order to make her male, so that she too may become a living spirit resembling you males. For every woman who will make herself male will enter the kingdom of heaven.[8]

Here the Gnostic writer, attributed to Didymos Judas Thomas (or Judas "the twin"), reveals his unconscious assumptions about masculine superiority. But a bald pronouncement that the writer assumes a norm of masculine superiority is too simplistic. This passage is an indication of the complexity of Hellenistic thought, and Judaic Dualism, regarding matters of human gender and divinity. Recent research, and translations of the Dead Sea Scrolls, would indicate that this duality is derived (both) from the teachings of such communities as the one at Qumran (which was Jewish), as well as from Hellenistic or Platonic thought.

Elaine Pagels notes, "Some gnostics, reasoning that as *man* surpasses *woman* in ordinary existence, so the *divine* surpasses the *human*, ..." Thus this passage "may be taken symbolically: what is merely human (therefore *female*) must be transformed into what is divine (the 'living spirit,' the *male*).[9]

While Pagels' explanation is illuminating, it is not adequate for this complex concept of dualistic thought, one in which the human who aspires to an elevated form of spirituality denies the body and ultimately possesses no sexual libido whatsoever. It is inadequate because it does not take into account the *habits of the mind* which underlie its assumptions. The male who wrote the Gnostic gospel mirrored cultural norms of the day when he wrote this text. The words of Jesus, like the words attributed to Jesus even in those gospel texts which are part of accepted canon, are ones derived from an oral tradition. They were words the writers put into the mouth of Jesus, and while they may even be relatively accurate, they are not "word-for-word" exact quotes. Such quotes are nonexistent.

Saint Augustine, particularly, grapples with this concept, writing about it in his now famous book entitled *Confessions*. He (at the insistence of his influential mother, Monica) rejected the concubine who had shared his life and given birth to his son, and decided "that no bodily pleasure, however great it might be and whatever light might shed lustre upon it, was worthy of comparison, or even mention, beside the happiness of the life of the saints."[10]

Gnostic dualism has greatly influenced the theology of the Christian church, even though the Church rejected Gnosticism as heretical. The concept of the body as inferior and the spirit as ascendent or superior is dominant in the writings of Gnostic authors (as well as those from the Judaic ascetic tradition and the Hellenistic philosophical arena). Paul, in his New Testament writings, was teaching a combination of Neoplatonic and Gnostic thought. One scholar writes, "In Paul the Greek view seems to have imposed itself on the Jewish."[11] His writings reflect his education at the feet of the Hellenistic (and/or Judaic Dualist) intellectuals of the day; his writings do not parallel the teachings of Christ! Certain Biblical scholars have long argued that Paul was, in fact, a Gnostic.

Augustine, in his adherence to these same dualistic notions of a split between soul and body, continues the negative Pauline tradition. From his linear perspective, however, we inherit a more insidious misunderstanding of "soul." Augustine believed the soul was the God imprinted image within the human, and named this "body-dominating soul," "the reasonable spirit ... the image of God in humans."[12] If the soul is reasonable, anything lacking in reason cannot be related to the soul. If the soul is God's imprint, and it is reasonable, then anything lacking in reason cannot bear the imprint of God. If woman is considered lacking in a capability for reason, being regarded as inferior and the embodiment of frail emotionality, then those who are male, and superior, and capable of reason are, by inference, the only ones who bear the true imprint of God and of God's holiness.

Women in early Christian communities, by accepting such theological understandings, believed their best chance of acceptance into the "Kingdom of Heaven" would come only through an emulation of the male. They were encouraged to do so, moreover, by the men who were the acknowledged authority figures. As an example, Leander of Seville, speaking to nuns about the higher qualities of virginity says such a woman is: "forgetful of her natural feminine weakness, she lives in *manly* vigor and has used virtue to give strength to her weak sex, nor has she become a slave to her body, which by natural law should be subservient to a man."[13]

The woman who acknowledges her body, who lives in the full vitality of womanhood, with all its sexual implications, can never aspire to the elevated level of spirit-filled living achieved by those who remain celibate. Such is the implication.

Peter R. L. Brown has published a comprehensive study which addresses practices of celibacy and virginity that were prevalent in Christian circles from the first to the fifth centuries C.E. This time in the history of Christianity is critical in that, "The acid polemics of the Fathers against the ecclesial leadership of

women and against their teaching and writing books
indicate that the question of women's ecclesial office
was still being debated in the second and third centuries C. E."[14] That a debate related to women's roles
even occurred is worthy of mention, even though it ultimately meant that the leadership of women was
deemed heretical.

Brown's book provides a plethora of examples of
the early Christian obsession with a dichotomized body
and spirit. Ascetics of both genders struggled to reach
a state of "*apatheia*," of sublime transcendence over
human passions, most particularly sexual passion. He
quotes one great Christian ascetic, Jerome, as lament-
ing:

> O how often, when I was living in the
> desert, in that lonely waste, scorched by
> the burning sun, that affords to hermits
> their primitive dwelling place, how often
> did I fancy myself surrounded by the
> pleasures of Rome ... though in my fear of
> Hell, I had condemned myself to this
> prison house, where my only companions
> were scorpions and wild beasts, I often
> found myself surrounded by bands of
> dancing girls. My face was pale with
> fasting; but though my limbs were cold as
> ice, my mind was burning with desire, and
> the fires of lust kept bubbling up before
> me while my flesh was as good as dead.[15]

Denial of one's bodily passions is obviously not a task
one undertakes without due trepidation! Augustine's
similar struggles mirror his (seemingly) overweening
preoccupation with sex and sexuality. The great women

ascetics of this time, however, embarked upon this sacred journey with great vigor and determination. Brown explores the central theme of a work written by Origen, an early Christian patriarch, (who argues against a polemic authored by a pagan Platonist, Celsus). Brown writes, "Virginity was presented as a privileged link between heaven and earth. For it was only through the 'holy' body of a virgin woman that God has been able to join Himself to humanity, thus enabling the human race to speak, at last, of Immanuel."[16] Origen, who reportedly had himself castrated in order to deny his own bodily passions, set great store in a celibate virginity. He saw it as a means of transformation and transcendence over "wantonness." Thus the holy state of virginity became the definitive place of superiority from which women could claim a kind of supreme Christianity.

Notes

1. Kahlil Gibran, *The Garden of the Prophet* (New York: Alfred A. Knopf, 1982), 30.
2. Lis Harris, *Holy Days: The World of the Hasidic Family* (New York: MacMillan Publishing Co., 1985), 140.
3. W. K. C. Guthrie, *The Greeks and Their Gods* (Boston: Beacon Press, 1955), 103.
4. Merlin Stone, *When God was a Woman* (London: Harcourt Brace Jovanovich, 1976), 157.
5. Clement of Alexandria, quoted in Virginia Burris' *Chastity as Autonomy* (Lewiston, NY: The Edwin Mellen Press, 1987), 66.

6. Soranus, *Gynaecia*, ed. J. Ilberg (Leipsig: Teubner, 1927), O. Temkin, Soranus' Gynaecology (Baltimore: Johns Hopkins University Press, 1956), 27.

7. Edward C. Whitmont, *Return of the Goddess* (New York: Crossroad Publishing Co., 1982), 127. (The emphasis is mine.)

8. James Robinson, ed., *The Gospel of Mary, The Nag Hammadi Library in English* (San Francisco: Harper & Row Publishing, 1988), 138.

9. Elaine Pagels, *The Gnostic Gospels* (New York: Random House, 1979), 67.

10. Saint Augustine, *Confessions* (New York: Viking Penguin Inc., 1961), 197.

11. Gerhard Kittel, ed., and Geoffrey W. Bromley, trans. and ed., *Theological Dictionary of the New Testament*, vol. 3 (Grand Rapids, Mich.: Wm. B. Eerdmans Publishing Co., 1965), 464.

12. Augustine, quoted in Elisabeth Moltmann-Wendel and Jürgen Moltmann's *Humanity in God* (New York: The Pilgrim Press, 1983), 93-94.

13. Leander of Seville, quoted in Rosemary Radford Reuther's *Sexism and God-Talk* (Boston: Beacon Press, 1983), 248.

14. Elisabeth Schüssler Fiorenza, *In Memory Of Her, A Feminist Theological Reconstruction of Christian Origins* (New York: Crossroad Publishing Co., 1985), 54.

15. Peter R. L. Brown, *The Body and Society: Men, Women and Sexual Renunciation in Early Christianity*, (New York: Columbia University Press, 1988), 375.

16. Ibid., 175.

6

The Legacy of Women Ascetics

"Call nothing ugly, my friend, save the fear of a soul in the presence of its own memories."

--Kahlil Gibran, *The Garden of the Prophet*[1]

The contrast between the Virgin Mary and Mary Magdalene became increasingly apparent as the patristic fathers tried to make an exact delineation between those women who could be regarded as *holy* and those who could not. While the mother of Jesus was seen as profoundly spiritual, in contrast, a woman who embodied the sensuality of a Mary Magdalene must be wanton and immoral. Thus, early women ascetics fled to the safety of a virgin spirituality. These women became known as "consecrated virgins" and as "daughters of Jerusalem."

One of the earliest of these women was Macrina,

who exerted considerable influence on her two brothers, Gregory of Nyssa and Basil of Caesarea, who
were, themselves, great Christian leaders of the day,
bearing the collective title of "the Great Cap-
padocians."[2] Macrina provides us with the quintessen-
tial portrait of a woman who began this tradition.
Growing up with her widowed mother, Emmelia,
Macrina participated in the day-to-day management of
a large household. She was psychically tied to her
mother in a singularly symbiotic way. Her brother,
Gregory, wrote that she was as close to her mother "as
if she were still in her mother's womb."[3]

When her fiance died, Macrina vowed never to
marry, and in time founded one of the first monastic
communities for women, persuading her mother to join
her in a life devoted to prayer, poverty and good works.
Gregory of Nyssa wrote of his sister and her followers:

> These women fall short of angelic and
> immaterial nature only insofar as they
> appeared in bodily form. ... Nor did she
> (Macrina) behave in any ignoble or wo-
> manish way. ... Nothing was left but the
> care of divine things, and the unceasing
> round of prayer and endless hymnody,
> coextensive with time itself, practiced by
> night and day.[4]

Here "angelic" qualities are equated with a demeanor
which denies one's womanhood, with its "ignoble" implications. The body is to be ignored and subjugated
into an ascetic sublimation whose only focus is upon
"divine things."

Of equal (or more) interest to readers of early
Christian history is the concept Macrina espoused which

identifies Christ as the divine bridegroom, to whom she is perpetually wed. Around her neck she "wore a ring containing what was supposedly a fragment of the Cross. This ring and its relic were also the pledge of the enduring presence of Christ, her true Bridegroom."[5] Out of this evolved the Roman Catholic practice (which is no longer favored) of anointing nuns as the "Brides of Christ." For Macrina this marriage to Christ was purely esoteric, attained through sexual abstinence, and denial of the body's passions, which she equated with "warts."[6]

Another historic woman ascetic, Teresa of Avila, takes a different, but also intriguing approach. Born in 1515, Teresa of Avila lived during a time when Spain enjoyed its zenith of imperial domination. She was a bright, sensitive young woman who at the age of twenty embraced a religious life with great fervor. Her denial of her bodily passions took on a psychosomatic form and she suffered from various kinds of physiological symptoms and physical ailments for the next twenty years of her life.[7] But then Teresa had a mystical conversion experience which created great change in her life. Theologian Rosemary Radford Ruether, describes this phenomenal occurrence in this way:

> At age forty she had a conversion experience that enabled her increasingly to assert herself as an independent person, defy her superiors, and become a leader and reformer of the Carmelite order in her own right. This conversion experience took the form of the establishment of a spiritual, erotic relationship with Christ as her lover who also gave her permission to defy the authorities of her Church and

society. ... The nuptial imagery of union
with Christ allowed Teresa to find a focus
for her own intellectual and erotic energies in this relationship and also to receive back from this relationship an ego
empowered to act with authority. Although she images Christ as male lover,
she also does not hesitate to use other,
maternal images, such as breasts over-
flowing with milk that nurtures the whole
community who journey toward this union
with Christ.[8]

While Macrina seems to be the initiator of Brides of
Christ, Teresa of Avila adds an unmistakably erotic
texture to women's ascetic history, an aspect which
would continue even though it was discouraged by the
church fathers. But the erotic aspects of Teresa's
experience cannot be separated from her understanding
of herself and her God in a spiritual, sensual, and
sexual way. The inextricable intertwining of spirituality
and sexuality is evident here and in the issues the
modern church still holds as problematic.

One other great woman ascetic adds an innova-
tive dimension to this picture. She is Julian of Norwich, a fourteenth century English anchoress, who lived
in a tiny cell-like dwelling attached to the parish church
in Norwich. She cannot escape her physical body, with
its concurrent vulnerabilities, since she prays:

I desired three graces by the gift of God.
The first was to have recollection of
Christ's Passion. The second was a bodily
sickness, and the third was to have, of
God's gift, three wounds. ... the wound of

contrition, the wound of compassion, and the wound of longing with my will for God.[9]

And God answers her prayers. In May of 1373 Julian is given her vision of Christ's Passion, a vision she then ponders for the next twenty years. This vision is followed by a succession of others during this period of time, visions which Julian described in glorious detail.

Julian's descriptions of her visions outraged church officials because she sees Christ as Holy Spirit-Mother. Here is an excerpt from one of her "showings":

> I saw and understood that the high might of the Trinity is our Father, and the deep wisdom of the Trinity is our Mother, and the great love of the Trinity is our Lord; and all these we have in nature and in our substantial creation. And furthermore I saw the second person, who is our Mother, substantially the same beloved person, has now become our mother sensually because we are double by God's creating, that is to say substantial and sensual. Our substance is the higher part, which we have in our Father, God Almighty; and the second person of the Trinity is our Mother in nature in our substantial creation, in whom we are founded and rooted, and he is our Mother of mercy in taking our sensuality. And so our Mother is working on us in various ways, in whom our parts are kept undivided; for in our Mother Christ we

profit and increase, and in mercy he re-
forms and restores us, and by the power
of his Passion, his death and his Resurrection he unites us to our substance.[10]

Historian Catherine Walker Bynum offers an explanation, or translation, of this vision when she writes:

Unlike earlier women, Julian saw motherhood as the completion of fatherhood, but
her theological position went well beyond
all earlier formulations, male and female.
To Julian, God's motherhood, expressed
in Christ, is not merely love and mercy,
not merely redemption through the sacrifice of the cross, but a taking on of our
physical humanity in the Incarnation, as a
mother gives herself to the fetus she
bears.[11]

While Bynum's understanding of Jesus' humanity is
valid, I believe she has missed the critical point in this
vision. Julian of Norwich is "shown" that there is no
separation between body and spirit, between "sensual"
and "substantial." She sees that Christ, "our Mother,"
means for us to understand that "our parts are kept
undivided." She tells us that the dualistic notion of a
flesh and spirit divided is wrong, because Christ has
"united us to our substance." With his Resurrection,
Christ gives us back our spirits, they are not separate
from the physicality of our human existence. Even as
we carry the image of God, our sensuality too is a
healthy and sacred aspect of our physical being, and of
our spiritual being.

Julian of Norwich is shown that there is a feminine entity who is "the deep wisdom of the Trinity" and "our Mother." The Motherhood of the Holy Spirit is an understanding derived from the Hebrew word for Spirit [*ruach*] which is feminine, as is the word for "Wisdom" in Hebrew [*chokma*].[12] So, too, in the Kabbalistic[13] tradition, the great Shekhinah is the feminine essence of God, and thus the "feminine principle in the Deity." She is that one who stood side by side with the creator when the world was formed, she is that one who participated when humans were made in the image of the deity ("Let *us* make humankind in *our* image, according to *our* likeness"[14]), she is that one who is the Holy Spirit of God.[15]

The *Shekhinah* carries connotations of holy mystery, of the very holiness of God. She is the feminine container for the mysterion that is God. In Kabbalistic thought, she is the manifestation of the *hidden* nature of God, in contrast to the *revealed* nature of God. Thus, "two basic attributes are contrasted with one another: God's 'holiness,' which denotes the presence of the *Shekhinah* in all things ... the hidden Kavod, and God's 'greatness' or 'sovereignty,' which has both appearance and size."[16]

That difference is like the difference between knowledge that is held at a rational, thinking level, and knowledge that comes from the intuitive, relational level. The *Shekhinah* (who carries the imagery of female) represents the intuitive, relational; the sovereign God (who carries the imagery of male) is perceived on a rational, linear plane.

My understanding of Julian's vision is also closely attuned to the earliest Hebrew concepts of the body and soul as representative of a totality which could not be separated. In the sacred breath of the deity who has imprinted humans with the image of itself, the em-

bodied spiritual breath empowers and emboldens the
created image in its totality, not in some esoteric portion thereof.

The critical factor in this understanding has to
do with the word in the original Hebrew, *"nephesh."*
When God breathes into the first human's nostrils the
divine breath, then that creature who inhales the breath
of life becomes a *nephesh*, "a living soul," "a living
being."

The Hebrew understanding here is the diametri-
cal opposite of the dualistic concept of separation
between body and spirit.   When human creatures receive the breath of life, and become living beings, "a
living soul is not put into one's body. The person as a
living being is to be understood as a whole and any
idea that one is made up of body and soul is ruled
out."[17] Furthermore, "a human being does not consist of
a number of parts [like body and soul and so on], but
rather is "something" that comes into being as a human
being by a quickening into life. ... To exist as a human
being then is to exist in undivided unity."[18] "The Old
Testament knows nothing at all of a separation of a
person's spiritual and corporeal components, it sees the
person as a whole."[19]

We are not fragmented parts of a whole, we are
holistic entities whose unity of soul and body has been
misunderstood and misinterpreted.   The majority of
religious and philosophical schools of thought in the
Near East (during the time when the canon was set for
the New Testament), including Gnostic thought and
Hellenistic philosophy, and not excluding Jewish Dualism and asceticism, each supported the concept of the
soul as ascendent over the body, or a flesh and a spirit
as divided. Just as human sexuality is not an exclusive
experience of the genitalia, but rather a sensuous un-

derstanding of body and soul as inextricably bound together as one; neither is human spirituality restricted to either/or interpretations by those who have set themselves up as the exclusive purveyors of the Truth. Human spirituality has suffered untold pain from such Truth, just as it has suffered untold pain from notions that the creation stories in the canon (the book of Genesis contains more than one) are the literal truth. I have used the anthropomorphic story of a Creator God in order to explain my understanding of the divine imprint within human beings. I do not accept the creation myths of the Old Testament as "literal" truth or as "inerrant," but my faith and my understanding of (my own and others') human spirituality is informed by their underlying, symbolic meaning. Like all mythological and symbolic texts, they point beyond themselves to a realm of divine mystery. I do not believe in a literal "virgin" birth for Jesus either, but that does not inhibit my ability to accept and embrace this man/God as a salvific model from whom I can understand my own human journey.

I believe that every human being has a deeply held divine imprint. Too often this God imprint has been taken by the institutional church and has been deformed and stunted in order to protect those who believed their's was the "manifest destiny" of leadership and control. This stance is derived from uninformed Biblical illiteracy, not true theological scholarship. As long as the Biblical text is used for such purposes, there will always be those who are set apart and marginalized, whether they be people of color, or homosexuals, or Jews, or women.

It cannot go unmentioned that the original Hebrew text from which this word *nephesh* is derived was written by a Biblical author who has been identified as J. The Old Testament has a number of authors, or strands; these writers are identified with letter designations, like P, E, R or D. The writer of the J material is an author who used the word Yahweh as a designation for God. [The letter J is derived from the German word Jahweh or its misspelled English translation into Jehovah.] The writings of J are believed to be the oldest strand in the Pentateuch.

In 1990 two respected Hebrew scholars presented the world with the audacious and surprising premise that this author, known simply as J, was a woman! J was a woman of the royal house, who lived during the time of King Rehoboam, son of King Solomon, (and grandson of King David). These authors who translate, and interpret, the writings of J note that "the investment, societal and individual, in the institutionalized misreading of J is extraordinarily comprehensive, since it is divided among Jews, Christians, Muslims, and members of the secular culture."[20] Suffice it to say, each entity they accuse of "institutionalized misreading" was, and is, an established patriarchy.

This author--who is nameless except for the designation J, like the other women whose stories have been distorted, or left unwritten, is the victim of historical prejudice. Without a conscious, intentional movement to correct this prejudicial understanding of women and their works, the tradition will continue. The visions of women must be held up to the light and examined, for they can enlarge the faith journey of many. They can speak to those who have tired of the dogmatic stance of the institutional church, and who have, to maintain their own psychic integrity, left it.

Another woman is given a vision akin to that of Julian of Norwich. But this woman's vision is given to her thirteen hundred years earlier. This woman is

Mary Magdalene and her vision is one she describes at Peter's request, saying, "What is hidden from you I will proclaim to you."[21]   When Mary had told the disciples her vision, some of them, including Andrew and Peter, criticized her and claimed the vision had no validity.

Peter's anger is greatest, and her confrontation with him is also detailed in *The Gospel of Thomas, Pistis Sophia,* and *The Gospel of the Egyptians.* The evidence of jealousy between Peter, who would assume a leadership role later, and Mary Magdalene, who has already been accorded inherent leadership (but whose leadership is denied her by those who manipulate the canon), is obvious in these extra-canonical accounts.

Admittedly, this vision also shows the Gnostic bias for the soul as ascendant over the flesh, and its apocalyptic tone is typical of early Jewish apocalyptic writings.   Interpretation of this text is further complicated by the loss of four pages from the text, pages which are crucial to its understanding. But it does give us a glimpse into a dimension of Christianity which allows Mary Magdalene to claim the place accorded her by Jesus, who says to her, "Blessed are you, that you did not waver at the sight of me."[22] The editors of the Nag Hammadi text note that:

> Peter and Andrew represent orthodox positions that deny the validity of esoteric revelation and reject the authority of women to teach. *The Gospel of Mary* attacks both of these positions head-on through its portrayal of Mary Magdalene. She is the Savior's beloved, possessed of knowledge and teaching superior to that of the public apostolic tradition.   Her superiority is based on vision and private

revelation and is demonstrated in her
capacity to strengthen the wavering disciples and turn them toward the Good.[23]

This woman, who returns to tell the disciples both of
the risen Christ and of her subsequent vision/dream, is
one whose life's story has been lost to modern women.
When even the broken pieces of it are recaptured, we
will have moved to a more enlightened understanding
of our own individual, and feminine, spiritual journey.

Medieval Christian women did not have a female role model, either. These early ascetics adopted
practices which were later evident in Judaic Kabbalism
and other (male) ascetic traditions. Fasting was one of
these practices; many of the women who were elevated
to the status of saints by the Roman Catholic church
would clearly be labeled "anorexic" in today's vernacu-
lar.[24] In addition to food deprivation, these women also
focused upon physical suffering as a transcendent method of attaining a higher level of spiritual connectedness with Christ. Spiritual perfection, achieved at the
cost of enormous suffering, became their goal.

In this suffering, denial of the body and its
physical needs was implicit. Elisabeth Schüssler Fiorenza writes that the religious communities of the day
"engendered a symbol system of theological legitimiza-
tion that seems to be strongly influenced by a negative
understanding of sexuality and of women's nature."[25]
The historic inheritance of body denial as equated with
spirituality, so that sensuality is (by implication) sinful,
is one which women who have been socialized in the
Western Christian tradition cannot avoid.

What impact does this have on the lives of
women who are still socialized in this way? This question cannot be answered without delving into the psy-

chological framework of these socialization patterns. Whereas, Veblen's *habits of the mind* theory allows us to understand that we continue archaic societal imperatives long "after the material conditions that gave rise to them have disappeared," we are still left with the complex nature of this sociological phenomenon.

Carl Jung's theory is helpful in understanding why the collective continues to cling to anachronistic imagery. According to Jung, the human psyche is made up of discernable layers, layers which not everyone holds in awareness. The uppermost level or layer of the psyche is the *conscious* level. It is that portion of the psyche of which we are most aware. In this layer are held cultural norms and social mores, our rational, linear perceptions of that which is deemed to be right or wrong. This is the level of the psyche most honored by the cultural and scientific world around us; it is the place from which technological knowledge is derived (and then deified). It is the place where codified church doctrine is held (and then elevated). The United States, as a rational, scientifically attuned culture, honors only this level of the psyche.

The next layer contains the *ego*. The ego comprises our identity as an individual; it is the "I" whom we believe ourselves to be. In the western culture, the ego has become synonymous with the totality of our human personality. The modern psyche has lost its ability to connect with the deep spirituality offered at lower, less-rational levels of the psyche. Thus the ego presents an obstacle to the lower, unconscious levels of the psyche, exercising an almost autonomous resistance to that which is held at the unconscious level.

Just below the ego is the layer which Jung labeled "the personal unconscious." It holds contents which have been repressed and suppressed during one's lifetime, those things we believe to be unacceptable and undesirable because we have been socialized to do so. At this level the *shadow* holds these sublimated contents, which are both spontaneously positive and repressively negative. Its contents are most usually understood in our projections, in that we often project onto others the contents of our *shadow,* while denying those same qualities within ourselves. Thus our positive shadow contents will be most evident to us in our best friend, while our negative shadow contents always appear in our worst enemy.

At the deepest level of the psyche is the "collective unconscious" or what Jung also termed "the objective psyche." Here the contents are primitive and instinctual, representing material we hold at birth, material which reflects thousands of years of social patterns and cultural understandings. Here the material is visceral and primordial, holding tremendous energy. This material is both distorted and enhanced by rational perceptions held at the conscious level, depending upon one's level of awareness. At this level of the psyche are held the *archetypes*, those "universal patterns or motifs which (come from the collective unconscious and) are the basic content of religions, mythologies, legends, and fairy tales. They emerge in individuals through dreams and vision."[26] These archetypes (which are not dissimilar from, but cannot be equated precisely with Veblen's *habits of the mind)* manifest themselves in the forms of humans or animals in our dreams and can be a rich resource for understanding our own psychic contents.

It is here, at this deepest level of the psyche, that imagery related to our respective gender roles is, on the one hand our richest source for that understanding, but on the other hand, a problematic and complex aspect of the human psyche. I believe that this level of the psyche holds the *mysterion*. It is the place where the soul cries out for authentic, fresh images of godness. The great themes of literature are here, but while we might be sympathetic enough to weep for the sacrifice of a Desdemona, we often refuse to allow ourselves to grieve for the corresponding archetype within ourselves.

There are many of these archetypal figures held in our objective or collective psyches, but the motifs of woman as *virgin*, or woman as *whore*, are those which are appropriate for understanding the roles women have had assigned to them. By definition these archetypes also reflect *cultural stereotypes*. These figures can literally be equated with the "historical"[27] Biblical figures of the Virgin Mary, who is the archetypal virgin, while Mary Magdalene has been assigned the role of the archetypal whore. While many women, particularly those who define themselves with a "feminist" label, reject cultural stereotyping, a failure to understand these unconsciously-held archetypes results in a continuing tension within individuals and between the collective of women and men.

The Virgin Mary carries an image of stainless sinlessness and elevated holiness. But Mary Magdalene's image is one of tainted sinfulness, with all the baseness implied in demon possession. The Virgin Mary stands outside human passion and rage and visceral feeling. But Mary Magdalene has been presented as one whose personality was cloaked in all three; the totality and particularity of her image has been primarily defined by these characteristics. The *critical* tension lies between the two opposites. Its dichotomy has left generation after generation of Christian women *uncon-*

sciously carrying this either/or belief about sexless-spirituality in opposition to sinful-sexuality.

The power of these archetypes is discounted or completely ignored by large portions of the population. Even psychologists who practice in the behavioral mode have a tendency to reject and discredit this actuality as valid. But all we need to do to understand its validity is to look at statistics about young women who are anorexics and bulemics. These women reflect an unconscious over-identification with Virgin Mary archetypal material, and at a deep level of the psyche believe that food deprivation will give them the same kind of spiritual ascendancy as a Catherine of Siena. While Catherine of Siena *may* have had a more conscious awareness of her body denial, these women are completely unconscious of, completely unaware of, the psyche's drive toward spiritual wholeness. Their denial takes the body to an extreme degree of gender ambiguity in that their menstrual periods cease, their bodies reach a point of emaciated thinness, and they begin to look like sick teenage boys. It is the ultimate expression of becoming like the male in order to *unconsciously* enter the Kingdom of Heaven, and its impetus is powerfully archetypal.

The one-sided imagery of a sexless Virgin Mary is the root of this unconsciously motivated impetus:

> The Christian image of the Virgin-Mother in her one-sided stainlessness excludes important elements of humanity and thus contributes to, rather than relieves, Christian misogyny. ... A humanly unreal virgin and mother, when taken literally and not as a symbol of spiritual self-renewal or self-birth ... can only contribute to hostility

toward real women, and confirm the threat that women presumably pose to masculine spirit in pursuit of a perfection defined in terms that virtually exclude a living relation to the feminine.[28]

Defined in this way, a "Virgin-Mother" is a mother without her basic humanity, one who flies in the skies of spirit (without authentic connectedness to body). Women who unconsciously fall in love with this imagery too often become the wasted starvelings who are now labeled anorexic.

The medical community has had to respond to the blatant starvation of numerous young women; research and health care for bulimics and anorexics is a modern phenomenon. The church also needs to understand the underlying psychological dynamics which create this phenomenon. These women have denied their womanhood, not because of a rational decision, but because of a primitive instinctual one, because "as the instincts are to the body, so are the archetypes to the psyche." The fact is the culture itself has denied women their authentic womanhood. We cannot ignore the archetypal evidence of food which becomes sacred, distorted into the means by which one becomes spiritually attuned. We have all inherited the archetypal patterns of those women who began the tradition. We share their obsessions and compulsions in the most unconscious and primordial ways.

Not only are women caught by their own archetypal either/or patterns, but the projections of (both) other women and men, regarding women's roles, create great conflict. The woman who becomes anorexic (and thus unconsciously identifies herself in the role of holy virgin) may have a sister who plays out the archetypal role of whore, in believing that her body is her only ticket to success. She unconsciously buys into a popular, media-aided image of herself as fragmented into parts, parts which are comprised of either beautiful breasts or great legs or an appealing rear end.

But the fragmentation into parts is accompanied by a desecration of her soul material in that she cannot perceive herself beyond the parts; she is a walking around piece of the whole. Without the beautiful breasts, or legs, or rear end, she perceives herself as a nothing, because she has completely lost touch with herself as a whole. In the case of the anorexic, all the awareness has gone to her head, while her body is sacrificed. In the latter case, all the awareness (such as it is) seems to flow out of one part of the body, while the head is sacrificed.

In my experience of knowing a woman whose sum totality of womanhood has been focused upon her large breasts, the split, itself, has resulted in a masculine dominated psyche. This woman has become a psychically "armored Amazon."[29] She is tough, aggressive, and independent. But, within that aggressive woman is the wounding that created the armoring in the first place. Ironically, legends of Amazon women declare that they "even removed their right breast so they could shoot arrows more effectively."[30]

In each case, the over-identification with an extreme archetype, an either/or pattern, has taken control, ruling the life of the individual. So many women in this culture struggle with body image and (not without consequence) with spirituality issues. Recent research has shown that far larger percentages of women, compared to men, have a distorted perception of their body image. This same research shows that girls as young as the age of ten begin to worry about their weight and agonize over going on diets, while their male counterparts seem relatively oblivious to body image. Such is the legacy of women ascetics, women who themselves were taught to deny their authentic femaleness.

Notes

1. Kahlil Gibran, *The Garden of the Prophet* (New York: Alfred A. Knopf, 1982), 27.

2. Justo González, *The Story of Christianity* (San Francisco: Harper and Row, Publishers, 1984), 181.

3. Peter R. L. Brown, *The Body and Society: Men, Women and Sexual Renunciation in Early Christianity,* (New York: Columbia University Press, 1988), 277.

4. Gregory of Nyssa, quoted in Rachel Hosmer's *Gender & God: Love and Desire in Christian Spirituality* (Cambridge, Mass.: Cowley Publications, 1986), 59. (The clarification within parentheses is mine.)

5. Brown, *The Body and Society,* 272-73.

6. Rachel Hosmer, *Gender & God: Love and Desire in Christian Spirituality* (Cambridge, Mass.: Cowley Publications, 1986), 60.

7. Catherine Romano, "A Psycho-Spiritual History of Teresa of Avila: A Woman's Perspective," in *Western Spirituality: Historical Roots, Ecumenical Routes,* ed. Matthew Fox (Notre Dame: Fides/Claretian, 1979), 274-278.

8. Rosemary Radford Ruether, *Womanguides, Readings Toward a Feminist Theology* (Boston: Beacon Press, 1985), 140.

9. Julian of Norwich, *Julian of Norwich: Showings,* trans. Edmund College and James Walsh (New York: Paulist Press, 1978), 125, 127.

10. Ibid., 294.

11. Caroline Walker Bynum, "... And Woman His Humanity": Female Imagery in the Religious Writing of the Later Middle Ages," *Gender and Religion: On the Complexity of Symbols,* ed. Caroline Walker Bynum, Stevan Harrell, and Paula Richman (Boston: Beacon Press, 1986), 266.

12. Jürgen Moltmann in ، Elisabeth Moltmann-Wendel and Jürgen Moltmann's *Humanity in God* (New York: The Pilgrim Press, 1983), 101.

13. Kabbalism is a form of Jewish mysticism. Its basic mode of apprehension is esoteric and mystical, as contrasted with the rational, linear perspective more typical of the Jewish Midrashim or the Talmudic commentaries. Kabbalism does not reject intellectual ways of understanding God, but rather seeks to extend those methodologies into the realm of mystery. Kabbalism relies upon both tradition and intuition, so that an understanding of God, and God's transcendence, is derived through introspection.

14. Genesis 1:26, *The New Revised Standard Version of The Holy Bible,* (Nashville: Cokesbury, 1990), 2.

15. Gershom Scholem, *Kabbalah* (New York: Dorset Press, 1987), 6, 17, 31-32, 35, 38. (The emphasis is mine.)

16. Ibid., 40.

17. Claus Westermann, *Genesis 1-11: A Commentary,* trans. John J. Scullion S. J. (Minneapolis: Augsburg Publishing House, 1984), 207.

18. Ibid., 206.

19. Ibid., 150.

20. Harold Bloom and David Rosenburg, *The Book Of J* (New York: Grove Weidenfeld, 1990), 11.

21. James Robinson, ed., *The Gospel of Mary, The Nag Hammadi Library in English* (San Francisco: Harper and Row Publishers, 1988), 525.

22. Ibid.

23. Ibid., 524.

24. The modern phenomenon of anorexia and bulimia needs to be understood in relation to this historical parallel. Jungian Analyst Marion Woodman has completed a definitive study on these conditions in her books entitled: *The Owl Was a Baker's Daughter: Obesity, Anorexia Nervosa and the Repressed Feminine* (Toronto: Inner City Books, 1980); and *Addiction to Perfection: The Still Unravished Bride* (Toronto: Inner City Books, 1982).

25. Elisabeth Schüssler Fiorenza, "Response to the 'Social Functions of Women's Asceticism in the Roman East,' by Antoinette Clark Wire," in *Images of the Feminine in Gnosticism*, ed. Karen L. King, (Philadelphia: Fortress Press, 1988), 327.

26. John P. Dourley, *The Psyche as Sacrament: A Comparative Study of C. G. Jung and Paul Tillich* (Toronto: Inner City Books, 1981), 115.

27. These figures are very much a part of the collective imagination and its assumptions of historical accuracy. Yet these women are depicted in the words of canonical writers who were writing decades after the actual events. History is rarely unbiased and objective; often it is subjective. The images of these women suffer from the notion that their depictions are accurate simply because their meager story is part of the narrative of accepted canon, the Bible.

28. John P. Dourley, *The Illness That We Are: A Jungian Critique of Christianity* (Toronto: Inner City Books, 1984), 61.

29. This designation is one used by Jungian Linda Schierse Leonard, in *The Wounded Woman: Healing the Father-Daughter Relationship* (Boston: Shambhala, 1985), 60-71.

30. Ibid., 60.

7

Jesus and Archetypal Wholeness

"I am a wanderer. Oftentimes it seems that I walk the earth among pygmies. ... But in truth I walk not among (humans) but above them, and all they can see of me is my footprints in their open fields."

--Kahlil Gibran, *The Wanderer: His Parables and Sayings*[1]

Males, too, have been psychically split apart by the power principles of the patriarchy. One theologian writes, "Patriarchy cut the male in half. It split him into a subject, consisting of reason and will, and an object, consisting of heart, feelings, and physical needs. He had to identify himself with the former and keep his distance from the latter. This isolated the male and brought about a certain self-hatred."[2]

"Reason and will" have been redefined and concretized into the only acceptable means for understanding God, but conversely as an explanation for our arrogant use of force and power. (The United States has long believed that only a male could act as its president, since a woman would not be willing to declare war.) The modern psyche of both genders bears the scars of anachronistic assumptions, ones that continue to push the male into a place of inauthentic masculinity, while women are taught to deny the very being of themselves.

What has any of this to do with theology? How can a closer look at what Mary Magdalene symbolizes elucidate a valid issue for theologians? These dynamics *cannot* be separated from theology, not if the church is going to function in the real world, a world filled with human frailties and pain. Addressing just these kinds of problems is where the church must take itself; these are the issues both women and men struggle to understand. A reformed understanding of theology insists that the church cannot isolate itself into some ascetic desert of scholarly understanding, holding its people at arm's length. A reformed theology enters into the lives of people in the same ways as Jesus of Nazareth, and in that visceral experience of the human, a new understanding of God can be realized.

While women need to reach this balanced place of knowing themselves as both sensual and spiritual (living in the same body), men need to address the corresponding archetypal material within themselves, so that they can become conscious enough to withdraw their either/or projections. One of the more visible aspects of these archetypal patterns has exploded through the media in recent years. Men who still cast women into extreme archetypal patterns (often seem to) choose the ministry as a vocation. Unfortunately these men are some of the most dangerous to women, simply because of their own distorted perceptions.

However, what *cannot* be forgotten, or simply side-stepped, is the historic role of the church. The church has helped to distort; it now needs to participate in the necessary healing process. While not every (male) minister who is guilty of this distortion is as visible as a Jim Bakker or a Jimmy Swaggart, male ministers who have "secret" affairs with their women parishioners are playing out time-honored archetypal patterns.

Jungian Robert Moore describes four masculine archetypes which can give both women and men a clearer understanding of their own interiority and illuminate the psychic forces which drive their actions. These archetypes are held within the deepest layers of the collective unconscious of *both* men and women; they are the king, the warrior, the magus (magician), and the lover.[3] I believe that Jesus lived out a complete integration of his own archetypes, thus representing the ultimate model of individuation. "Individuation is the process of the ego discovering, conversing with, and relating to the objective psyche, and realizing that it is subject to this more comprehensive psychic entity."[4] These archetypes were as much a part of Jesus as they are to any other human. By comparison, his life then becomes a model for wholistic living.

The "king" archetype represents that one who was the "center of the universe, one who provided order."[5] In his very being he represented the "source of creativity" and of phallic divinity. He was a king whose fertility was assumed; without it his power was diminished to nothingness. The image of the king represented a "centeredness that was calm,"[6] endowed with potent quietude, and content with itself and its world. This archetype is critical to order in the world; without it the world descends into chaos.

While the Christian church has long used the

title *King* for Jesus, it has bestowed the title on the one hand, while stripping it of its integrity and power on the other. The church has emasculated Jesus. By denying him his normal, human sexuality, those early Christians who wrote the canon set up a dynamic which has created an atmosphere for cultural and global chaos. Those who continue this tradition by insisting upon a strict and literal translation of the text are inconsistent. They want to espouse the creativity, the power, and the potency of this Jesus, but they have ripped away the sexuality that must accompany such potency.

An emasculated king at the center of the universe means that the world has been robbed of its potent creativity, only to try to recapture it through technological or scientific means. But, phallic potency cannot be replaced with technology. Phallic potency is primordial and instinctual in its wisdom. Computers have no connection with, no understanding of instinct. Far more often this archetype is evident from its shadow side. The negative/shadow side of this archetype is manifested in every tyrant, every despot who ever ruled through the use of terror. It is Adolph Hitler, Joseph Stalin, and Saddam Hussein. The institutional church functions from the shadow side of this archetype each time it uses power to oppress, instead of to empower. The patriarchal church, at its worst, is the lived shadow side of the king archetype. A Committee on Preparation for the Ministry of the Word and Sacrament, functioning from an authoritarian, dictatorial model, is living out the shadow aspects of this archetype.

Jesus, however, embodies the king archetype with unparalleled grace. He is calm in the face of danger; serene when taunted by those who are the orthodox leaders of the day. He is creative when food is scarce and the hungry are numerous. He is ultimately and completely at ease with himself and his surroundings. He is the embodiment of order, refusing to indulge in physical warfare. Instead, he speaks of peace, he offers peace of soul and heart. He brings order out of chaos, he is order personified and magnified.

The "warrior" archetype embodies a "radical commitment to transpersonal loyalty and service." This archetype is one of intentionality; without it no one ever completes a doctoral dissertation! The warrior archetype carries "enormous capacity for discipline, self-abnegation, and courage in facing insurmountable odds."[7] The warrior can "stand pain," much pain in order to achieve its purposes. The warrior is that "capacity to radically relativize one's relations in the service of higher loyalties."[8]

Again, the Christian church has long used warrior language to associate itself with Jesus. This language has been literal in the history of the church; it is constellated in the crusades or "Holy Wars," the inquisitions, and the witch hunts of the early-eighteenth century. Those who still speak of doing "spiritual warfare" in relation to the church are speaking from a literalized understanding of this archetype. Moore notes that, "the less developed humans are, the more prone they are to literalize and act out of archetypal structures."[9] At its worst, this archetype has been concretized in wars waged by countries who regard themselves as truth bearers. Too often, Christians have been among those who have fought such wars, because the shadow side of this archetype refuses to acknowledge "the atrocities it commits."

Jesus, a man/God who is truly warrior, lived out this archetype in a balanced, wholistic way. He is thoroughly committed to his work, even to setting aside family in order to complete it, proving his ability to see himself in relation to a transcendent loyalty. He is capable of warrior discipline, even though his disciples are not. He tolerates extreme pain, even death, to honor his fidelity to his God. Only a man/God who embodied the warrior could have entered the depths of primordial mystery. When Jesus descended into hell he did so through this archetype.

The archetype of "magus," sometimes known as wizard, sometimes labeled magician, is an archetype of potent awareness and insight. It is the most introverted of the archetypes and in an extroverted world has not received much attention. It is the "analytical mind that understands dynamic energy and energy patterns;" it knows "what is safe to do and what is not." This archetype is the one that faces forces of great power, even "celestial hierarchies,"[10] and recognizes both the evil and the good in them.

The Christian church (and the American culture) has projected this archetype onto its leaders, preachers, professors, and scientists, most of whom are incapable of living it! Those among this group who have falsely inflated egos believe themselves capable when they are not. Instead, if their ego inflation is grandiose enough, they function from the shadow side of this archetype in alarming ways, setting up their little realms, and wielding power from its shadow aspects, rather than from a place of authentic wisdom.

The shadow side of this archetype is manifested in unconscious power drives and in an overweening need to control, particularly those it has defined as "inferior." It is speaking when pastors use their acquired "knowledge to manipulate, not liberate."[11] It speaks each time a pastor (or the institutional church) lays claim to an exclusive patent on the intellectual knowing and defining of God's image for a congregation. The shadow side of the magus is most obvious in those who believe that only rational and precise methods of interpretation can be applied to the canon. Any suggestion that new understandings can be derived from extra-canonical sources, and from other methodologies, is refuted by the shadow side of this archetype.

Jesus, however, is the living model of a centered magus archetype. He used this archetypal power in his debates with the Pharisees in the temple, verbal sparring matches that were filled with his extraordinary insight. This was the archetype that came into play when embodied demons cried out their understanding of him and his divine identity. This archetype was evident each time he responded to those who accused him of sedition, even treason. It was the wisdom manifested in his silences, as well as his rebuttals to unjust condemnatory claims against him.

The archetype of "lover" *is* the Jesus of the gospel accounts. This archetype is that one which recognizes "the value in, and appreciates,"[12] those who are marginalized and thrust into an outgroup. To love without judging, without manipulation, and without compensatory or complimentary reaction is the positive side of this archetype. This love, though, is not that "agape" love held up by theologians as the purest kind of spirit-bound God-love. It must have a balancing eros component, or it is shallow and flat. This archetype is the multi-dimensional lover, one not robbed of its erotic qualities.

The Christian church has long struggled with the tensions created by this powerful archetype. It has been unbelievably creative in its misunderstanding of this archetype and has forced inconsistent creedal information upon its followers in an (unconsciously destructive) process.   One theologian has said, "The Christian Church has had an exclusive focus on the genitals as comprising all of human sexuality. ... The chasm between the biological sciences and theological sciences continues to cause, rather than heal, much human suffering."[13]

Thus, the church has defined the love of God as one of *agape*, while the love of humans is *eros*. The delineation between these two, derived from the original Greek of the New Testament, is not an indication of the being or life of Jesus. Nor is Greek the language that reflects Jesus' "true" words; he spoke Aramaic, not Greek. The delineation is, rather, evidence of the dualistic and Hellenistic influences that permeate the writings of the canon. As a result, the eros principle of this archetype has been relegated to the shadow places in the psyche, where it is lived out and/or projected onto others. It is acted out in a pathological way; it is literalized in the promiscuity of clergy.

Jesus lived this archetype in the fullest understanding of its richness and wholeness. He sought out those who were considered "unclean" by the followers of Judaic law. He ate meals with tax collectors; he touched lepers. He saw within each person the imprinted image of God, beneath the warts, beneath the ravages of leprosy, beneath the surly countenance. He saw and valued every person for their unique beingness, not for their position, not for the power they held, not for their physical appearance. The power of this love is the power of the Christian church as it should be. It is the love that Jesus held up to the light and exemplified in immeasurable ways. And among all those he met and came to know, he loved Mary Magdalene with a love that has been recorded and then declared heretical!

The institutional church and modern theological education, with its rational, linear perspective, has pushed into the minds [and hearts] of its parishioners and seminarians the image of a "god who stares down with his 'thou shalts' writ in stone, ... he keeps everything concrete and literal." [14] The (earlier) mystery (i.e., *mysterion*), while acknowledged almost as an aside, is not part of the primary focus. Instead, the overweening focus is upon a rational, linear perspective of God, a God who is apprehended through doctrinal, dogmatic theological understandings.

In this process, there is a danger that the average church member or theological student will give credence only to that which can be defended from a rational, analytical perspective. It is the unfortunate legacy we carry from a time known as "The Enlightenment." Sadly enough, when the archetypes held deep in the collective unconscious layer of the psyche are not honored, they are acted out anyway, but unconsciously (to which the Swaggarts, Bakkers, numerous Presbyterian pastors, and Catholic priests of the world can attest).

As I discussed the research for this book with a friend who is very interested in its psychological dimensions, she described a relationship which is a perfect example of the archetypal patterns I have discussed. A woman who is a fellow student (with her at a large university) had a passionate affair with the pastor who officiated at her father's funeral. My friend described this woman as a "quiet, mousy type with pursed lips," a woman who was driven by perfectionism, whose external sensuality seemed to be completely repressed. But, what happened when her father died? What unconscious action did she take when the authoritarian male who had cast her into a Virgin Mary archetypal mold died? The minister who preached her father's funeral became her sexual partner. She had sexual intercourse with the man who came to bless her father on his way! This quiet, mousy woman (who had heretofore carried the Virgin Mary projection] was driven by a powerful, opposite archetypal drive. She unconsciously descended into the whore archetype and acted from it.

Another woman whom I know had a "secret affair" with her minister, one that lasted twenty years. During this period of time she became pregnant and was forced to abort the baby as the only viable option. When her "secret lover" ultimately obtained a divorce, he did not marry her. He married, instead, the young secretary who had come to work in the church office. The woman who had the long-standing *secret* relationship was unceremoniously dumped, like yesterday's garbage. The quiet, mousy woman (in the previous illustration) was also dumped in a similar manner.

When one explores the primordial forces at work in these two examples, it is not inconsequential that these two affairs were also *secret.* The men who participated in them could only have conducted them in that way. The pivotal piece of this whole puzzle has more to do with *sacred* than with *secret.* While these men would not have had rational explanations for their actions, they reflect, in those actions, an over-identification with their own archetypal material, and of their projection of archetypal images onto these women.

The church that holds up the Virgin Mary as an icon for ideal womanhood pushes normally sensuous women into the role of mistress. The more literal the belief in this Virgin Mary notion, the greater the danger that male clergy will continue to objectify sensual women. With this objectification comes un-conscious erotic projection, an unhealthy projection which is often acted out.

In this twisted acting-out, the perpetrators take an act--sexual intercourse--and unconsciously bring it into a sacred arena. In so doing they are unconsciously playing out an over-identification with their deeply held, and ego-inflated, notions of themselves as a King or God figure, or even as a Savior. But, the Savior with whom these men have identified themselves is not overtly acknowledged as sexually active; a chaste and celibate character for this Savior has been presented. The sexual component of this Savior's human per-sonality has been pushed into the hidden, *secret* places of the collective psyche; the institutional church has forbade any other interpretation of the canonical text.

These men, schooled in theology and ethics, carry their congregations' collective projection of ideal moral leader. Nevertheless they take themselves and their *secret* sexual partners to a terrible place of psycho-logical and spiritual degradation. This is a pheno-menon which cannot be explained using behavioral psychological theory or the intellectual constructs of professional ethics. It is beyond the scope of such methodologies, because its cause, its underlying stimu-lus, is primordial and held at the deepest level of the unconscious.

The participants in these two examples have unconsciously taken the ordinary and made it into a mysterious ritual. It is the same kind of compulsion which drives alcoholism and workaholism. There is a crossover point, when the individual (who is uncons-cious of this internal world) translates the ordinary into the divine, when that which had been a *secret* also becomes that which is *sacred.* But "every secret is pro-

pelled by hidden inner forces toward human consciousness, and for this reason evil deeds eventually emerge
into the awareness of humanity in general or someone
in particular."[15] The actions of the individuals in these
two examples, both the men and the women, were
driven by their unconscious need for completion, for
spiritual wholeness. Their lack of an awareness of this
psychic, soul-level need caused them to act out of their
archetypal impetus.

That lack of awareness denotes a cultural morality based on extroverted, outwardly focused compli-
ance. It is an endorsement of doing what is right
because, otherwise, "What will people say?"   This
morality suffers from its own preoccupation with the
deeds of others and its need to assess whether those
actions are right or wrong. Such morality, because of
its external focus, excludes self-knowledge from the
equation, when this awareness of oneself is critical to a
higher, wholistic form of morality.

It must be stated that clergy labor under the
superhuman, and perfectionistic, projections cast upon
them from the canon, which declares: "Now a bishop
must be above reproach, married only once, temperate,
sensible, respectable, hospitable, an apt teacher, not a
drunkard, not violent but gentle, not quarrelsome, and
not a lover of money. He must manage his own household well, keeping his children submissive and respectful in every way--for if someone does not know how to
manage his own household, how can he take care of the
church? ...   Moreover, he must be well thought of by
outsiders, so that he may not fall into disgrace and the
snare of the devil."[16]

When clergy make the unfortunate mistake of
trying to live out this idealistic model, they deny the
very aspect of themselves that will not be denied. The

shadow will call forth the worst in us when we deny it; because then we will usually go out and project it onto another. Jungian theologian John Sanford points out that, "There are few people more dangerous in life than those who set out to do good. It can even be said that when we try to exceed our capacity for natural goodness we bring about evil, not more good, because our unnatural stance generates an accumulation of darkness in the unconscious."[17]

Too often the clergy, in trying to appease or heal the wounding from their birth father or mother, enter church-related vocations for just this purpose. The negative father/mother complex is *not* healed in this way, but more often is constellated and projected outward onto those who are parishioners. Affairs abound when either the oedipal or the electra complex is unconsciously activated, and then the collective shadow of the congregation will be unleashed in response.

Those who condemn the hypocritical aspects of Christianity often point to the false piety exhibited by those who fill both church pulpits and pews. Such piety is mawkish and insipid, wrapped up in itself, and displayed with pseudo-humble sentimentality. This shallow, artificial piety has become a persona label, a mask of Christianity.

The very socialization process itself calls up a persona mask. Early in life humans learn to conceal, or mask, their feelings of humiliation, or fear, or anger, when they are in the powerless years of childhood. That mask slips down over the face throughout one's lifetime whenever one is confronted with these same feelings. Their impact is cloaked beneath the false face presented to the world. The persona mask of Christianity is one of pious goodness, one of purity, one of perfectionistic, sexless idealism. It is a mask projected onto clergy, even when they do not accept the projection. But, when they are unconscious enough to accept the projection, God help them!

The institutional church has participated in this development of the Christian persona, in this splitting of the conscious and the unconscious. Its canon has told male clergy (or "bishops") to "manage [their] own households well, keeping (their) children submissive and respectful in every way--for if someone does not know how to manage his own household, how can he take care of the church?" Its patriarchal traditions have led males to isolate themselves into an egocentric place of reason and will, set over against its opposite relational, feeling component. Males then believe the former is the superior norm, thus relegating the latter to a place of inferiority. "This division in the male is reflected and takes an aggressive form in the male subjugation and domination of the supposedly 'frail,' 'emotional,' and 'physical' woman."[18]

The women who (in recent years) are becoming more aware of themselves as sacred vessels, are refusing to be abused in this way and are bringing this carefully concealed *secret* into a clarified focus. Women who have been abused by clergy are more willing to come forward and name their abusers than ever before. The betrayal that has occurred in countless pastor/-parishioner affairs is exacerbated because it is not simply a betrayal of body or even marital covenant. The spirit cannot be separated from the experience of the body, and this intertwined betrayal heaps guilt on top of vulnerability.

Furthermore, it is a betrayal by one who carries the projection of leader for God, sacred covenant definer, and ultimate counselor. While this designation is one born out of an imbalanced historical projection, anyone who claims to speak on behalf of God, who is called to lead a community of faith, thus has access to the deepest, most profound secrets of those who come seeking counsel. The woman who is cajoled into a sexual liaison with this male leader, comes away from such an encounter with a fragmented soul, and a misunderstanding of the who, and what, and why of God. Her personal connectedness to her own God is shattered, often never to be recovered.

A three-fold sociological dynamic may become part of this drama, if the woman is bold enough to accuse her male pastor of sexual harassment or abuse. The church, acting to protect itself (whether consciously or otherwise) responds in ways that "mitigate perfect justice." The one who brings the accusation to a public arena will often face an institutional reaction that is prone to "shoot the messenger," or will "misname the problem," or "blame the victim."[19] All these responses are ones which discount the anger and pain and abuse in an effort to maintain the church's reputation.

All these dynamics feed out of a patristic understanding of justice for women. One clergywoman who was an advocate for numerous women who had been abused by the same pastor writes, "I finally realized that women will never find perfect justice in a patriarchal institution. We can only expect approximate justice, not because people are incapable of something more, but because patriarchy will not allow anything more."[20]

The split between sexuality and spirituality, and the duality set up by the influence of Hellenistic thought and Jewish Dualism, has caused untold pain among those who are its inheritors. When sex is split off and reduced to a place of inferiority in comparison to spirituality, the body/spirit is unconsciously damaged in the process. The Pauline, and pseudo-Pauline, texts from the New Testament have contributed immeasurably to this destructive heritage. These texts have called up the split by telling Christians to be "good" not conscious; they have imprisoned their followers, not set them free. Reading beyond, beneath, and around the canon leads the reader to further questioning of the purposes and motivations of its authors.

Notes

1. Kahlil Gibran, "The Other Wanderer," *The Wanderer: His Parables and Sayings* (New York: Alfred A. Knopf, 1981), 92. The inclusive language change is mine.
2. Elisabeth Moltmann-Wendel and Jürgen Moltmann, *Humanity in God* (New York: The Pilgrim Press, 1983), 113.
3. Robert Moore, "Healing the Masculine" (Lecture delivered at the C. G. Jung Institute in Chicago, 1981).
4. Ann Belford Ulanov, *The Feminine in Jungian Psychology and in Christian Theology* (Evanston, Ill.: Northwestern University Press, 1971), 71.
5. Robert Moore, "Healing the Masculine" (Lecture delivered at the C. G. Jung Institute in Chicago, 1981).
6. Ibid.
7. Ibid.
8. Ibid.
9. Ibid.
10. Ibid.
11. Ibid.
12. Ibid.

13. Michael Peterson, quoted by Jason Berry in *Lead Us Not Into Temptation* (New York: Doubleday, 1992), 204.

14. Marion Woodman, *The Pregnant Virgin: A Process of Psychological Transformation* (Toronto: Inner City Books, 1985), 9.

15. John Sanford, *Evil: The Shadow Side of Reality* (New York: Crossroad, 1981), 107.

16. I Timothy 3:2-7, *The New Revised Standard Version of The Holy Bible* (Nashville: Cokesbury, 1990), 300-01.

17. Ibid., 65.

18. Moltmann-Wendel and Moltmann, *Humanity in God*, 113.

19. Marie M. Fortune, *Is Nothing Sacred?* (San Francisco: Harper San Francisco, 1989), 120.

20. Ibid.

8

Jesus, Mary Magdalene, and Projection

"I go, but if I go with a truth not yet voiced, that very truth will again seek me and gather me, though my elements be scattered throughout the silences of eternity, and again shall I come before you that I may speak with a voice born anew out of the heart of those boundless silences."

--Kahlil Gibran, *The Garden of the Prophet*[1]

Did the human Jesus and Mary Magdalene have a sexually intimate relationship? Were they husband and wife? In order to understand the archetypal material discussed in this paper, I will argue that they did have such a relationship. Here I am arguing that such a physical, sexual relationship did exist for the sake of this study and its contents. The itinerant rabbi Jesus was most unusual if he was not married, since that was the cultural norm of the time. To my mind, the actuality of this particular relationship is less important than the deeply held psychological dynamics which are evident in the collective unconscious. I will argue that this secret marriage of a man/God has been carefully protected by those who set the canon; the resultant influence on the church has perpetuated a norm for denying the body and defaming sexuality.

The scene in the garden, when Mary comes face to face with the resurrected Christ, is illuminating. When Jesus calls her by name, and she fully recognizes him, her first reaction is to rush to embrace him. But, for a Jewish woman in this time in history to embrace a man, she would have had to be his wife. Jewish codes of behavior forbade this kind of intimate action on the part of the woman, unless she was the man's wife, and even then it was a private gesture.[2] While the historical tradition makes a point of protecting both the full humanity and the divine character of Jesus, at the same time it has denied that Jesus could (or would) have been normally intimate.

If we look at the Gnostic passages about Mary Magdalene and Jesus, however, a more complete picture emerges. A relationship between a teaching rabbi, Jesus, and his female follower, (and wife) Mary Magdalene arises out of the Gnostic text. For Mary to accompany Jesus, as even accepted canon makes apparent, she would have had to be Jesus' wife.

Jewish rabbis were not single men; they gathered male students or disciples around them, and their single status would have been suspect in a culture that had set itself apart from the homosexual practices of the Greco-Roman culture. The Jewish community was extremely homophobic, and thus Jewish rabbis were usually married. It would have been against this cultural "norm" for Jesus to remain single.

When Mary Magdalene speaks to the person whom she believes to be the gardener, and asks to claim the body of Jesus, she is exercising her societal right as the next of kin.[3] She would not have asked to claim the body unless she had been the wife of Jesus. It would not have been unusual, or against the mores of the Jewish society, for a man to claim the body. After all, even the canon gives Joseph of Arimathea that privilege, but it would have been extremely unacceptable for any woman, other than Jesus' wife, to do so.

The notion of a married Jesus essentially completes and fulfills the teaching that Jesus was "fully and completely human" and makes him more accessible to our own human experience. In no way does it diminish his divine nature, but rather, it enhances it. Jesus cannot be "fully human" without the "lover" archetype, with all the rich, erotic components implied by this archetype. This archetype is essential to feeling, and Jesus was surely a man who felt deeply. Without this archetype he would have been incapable of feeling. If Jesus has experienced marriage, then God has experienced marriage, thus elevating this experience between women and men, giving it a divine coloration and affirming it as good. It then can be a truly holy covenant between two people, not primarily a social institution designed to legitimate the patriarchy.

The informed theologian who would look behind the canonical text and search for its hidden meaning, must then ask: How could Mary Magdalene *not* be the wife of Jesus? Was, as Bishop John Shelby Spong asks, the marriage at Cana Jesus' marriage?[4] If Mary Magdalene was the wife of Jesus, why has this important information been withheld from the canon?

I believe that Mary Magdalene's relationship as Jesus' wife has been kept *secret* for two thousand years. Those who were inculcated with the ideals of a Greco-Roman world, those who could only view the spirit as ascendent and superior to the body, believed this information must not be revealed in the canon. It *must* be kept *secret*. Its very secrecy is related to a core of belief in spiritual superiority and physical/bodily inferiority. Since it is information that has been held as secret, it has fallen into the mysterious realms of visceral, primitive psychic material known as the "collective unconscious." And there, like all *sacred/secret* things, it is protected with great intensity.

The men who, in this day and age, jeopardize themselves (and their churches) by indulging in secret encounters are playing out a dark and suprapersonal archetype. It is the shadow side of Jesus, a physical, sexual side that is normal and natural to the human condition. Because it has *not* been acknowledged, Jesus' sexuality is cast into the shadow and repressed out of conscious awareness. This side of the human Jesus has been denied by the church (and society). Clergy who have sexual relations with their parishioners are driven by this shadow and archetypal energy. It is a powerful energy, made even more powerful by its denial.

While the church has delegated unto itself the task of defining sin, too often it looks the other way when one of its own descends into this territory. Those who unconsciously act out their archetypal drives do so out of narcissistic egocentricity, but also from a failure to understand their own unconscious, obsessive identification with an archetype. The New Testament would have used the word "hubris" for such a sin, in that it entails "the arrogant setting up of the ego in place of God. The image the word conveys is of an ego that observes no boundaries, limits, or laws, but is completely dominated by egocentric attitudes and passions."[5] Here the ego is being driven, and in fact has been totally sublimated to, the raging archetype that is the shadow side of Jesus. If Jesus cannot be sensual, or normally and humanly sexual, then that quality descends into the archetypal realms of the collective psyche, where it is called up, and acted out, by unconscious individuals. Then the acting out, itself, is denied.

I believe the historical church, by externalizing and concretizing the entity who is identified as Satan (or the Devil) in the New Testament, has taken the shadow side of Jesus and used it as an excuse for projection. That projection has been unconsciously cast upon Mary Magdalene, and her female inheritors.

Jesus, however, did not disclaim his own shadow. When the three synoptic gospels declare that he went into the wilderness where he was tempted by the Devil or Satan, they set up a scenario for literal translators to believe in an external figure who represents evil, one who is evil personified. But, what reasonable adult would, in this modern age, declare that they had spent forty days in the desert where they were tempted by an identifiable entity known as Satan! People would immediately ask what kind of drugs they were taking!

Each of the three synoptic gospels indicates that Jesus was impelled into this temptation experience by the "Spirit." The Markan text (in its original Greek) uses the word "thrust" (often found in English translations as "driven by") to imply the power of the Spirit at work. To be *thrust* into the wilderness by the Spirit is to be pushed into this experience with incontestable force. I believe each human being is pushed into an encounter with her/his own individual shadow. We do not meet the Devil, nor do we meet Satan on this journey toward individuation. We meet our own internal, repressed energy held in the shadow. That meeting with the shadow, in my mind, comes from the impetus of the Spirit. When we meet and learn to integrate our own suppressed material, both negative and positive, material dwelling within the shadow, then we are empowered to a larger, more humane understanding of the richness and power of the divine. Then we begin to apprehend, even if only partially, a personal God image.

One of the grand old theologians of the Presbyterian Church, John Calvin, has written that such contemplation is vital to our knowing of both God and ourselves. In his definitive body of theological writings, John Calvin begins with a chapter subtitled, "Without knowledge of self, there is no knowledge of God."[6] Calvin goes on to write in this same subsection, "The knowledge of ourselves not only arouses us to seek God, but also, as it were, leads us by the hand to find him."[7] Calvin writes that we are lead to such understanding because each human being has "implanted" within "an awareness of divinity."[8] This awareness, the editor notes, is a "numinous awareness of God."

Even though Calvin was trained as a lawyer, he writes, "we are called to a knowledge of God, not that knowledge which, content with empty speculation, merely flits in the brain, but that which will be sound and fruitful if we duly perceive it, and if it takes root in the heart."[9] This heart-level knowing of God is key for Calvin, who concludes, "we need not seek [God] far away, seeing that he dwells by his very present power in each of us." Calvin's God was not an externalized projection who was perceived only on a rational, linear level. The God of whom Calvin wrote was one of "mysterium tremendum,"[10] a God whose "essence is incomprehensible."[11]

To spend the necessary reflective time in meeting, understanding, and integrating one's shadow is modeled by Jesus. Jesus, in those forty days in the wilderness, did not converse with a little horned being dressed in red and carrying a pitchfork. I believe that Jesus spent forty days in the wilderness reacting to his own internal (and very human) shadow. His wise responses to the shadow's temptations were evidence of his conscious ability to own the shadow and not be enveloped by it or driven by its grandiose, inflated demands. And yet, the church has denied that he would have possessed this normal, human aspect, even in the face of its doctrine which declares him to be "fully human." It is small wonder that unconscious male clergy descend into shadow places, where they act out of this secret shadow energy.

What about the women who allow themselves to be drawn into secret affairs with clergy? I believe they, too, are caught in (both) their own archetypal drives, as well as the projections of *whore* onto them. It is not insignificant that the ministers (in the two examples I have used) dumped their secret partners, nor that they did not make their relationships legitimate. Society has ordained the marriage covenant as sacramental; it carries this unconscious assumption, even in those protestant denominations where it is not a sacrament. Thus, the male minister, who in his priestly function conducts such marriage services, is more accountable than the laity for breaking (his own and others) marriage vows. To do so is an unconscious acting out of shadow material, and it is the equivalent of "stepping out" on God.

The woman who is cast into the stereotypically rigid model of whore cannot be acknowledged as good enough for marriage, a sacred and protected social institution. She always falls outside those unyielding, fixed parameters. She is *sinful*; she is the woman as tempter personified!   But in her psyche, in her own unconscious way, she is having sexual intercourse with the ultimate representative of the divine, a *man of God*. If her *God projection* onto her partner is extreme, she may unconsciously believe he is her only means to salvation. But sadly, what he pours into her body is not redemption, but his own hideous distortion of archetypal material.[12]

Nevertheless, the distortion of sensuality which became evident in the second century has continued its unfortunate legacy into our twentieth century lives. Without an understanding of that legacy, and its negative impact, we cannot hope to heal the wounds it has subsequently inflicted.   One of the women theologians who has written about our absence of healthy attitudes regarding the feminine is Ann Belford Ulanov.   I believe her books should be required reading for theological students of both genders.   Dr. Ulanov, the Christine Brooks Johnson Professor of Psychiatry and Religion at Union Theological Seminary in New York City, explores the relationship between religion and psychology.

Ulanov indicates that the antagonism between the genders in today's culture is symbolic of the polarity between the conscious and the unconscious levels of the psyche. While the conscious level, with its concomitant rational, linear processes is elevated to a superior level in our technological age, the unconscious level of the psyche, with its visceral primordial contents, is either denigrated or ignored.   This continues the legacy of perceiving men as superior and rational and women as inferior and irrational.

Ulanov makes two points which are appropriate for this particular study.   The first has to do with "the libido, Jung's term for the psychic energy which directs and motivates the personality." She says that the libido, "is the dynamism of the life process as manifested in the psychic sphere. To give attention to, to value, to be interested in something are all expressions of libido. The more value an object is felt to have, the more libido has been invested in it."[13]

The libidinal energy expended by early church fathers in both denying, defining, and setting rigid guidelines about the expression of sexuality is an indication of its unconscious value to them. The key word is *unconscious.* The contemporary church is no less obsessed with these same issues. The Presbyterian Church, U.S.A. (and its mainline counterparts) have discussed abortion and homosexuality ad nauseam, and continuing studies have been commissioned. These new studies follow on the heels of other recently commissioned ones which were rejected. But, the Presbyterian Church is rather infamous for its belief in the work of commissions, even if the issues addressed are not likely to be resolved in this way.

The libidinal energy in the modern organized church may be roiling beneath the surface of a worship ritual. A remarkable (unconscious) outbursting of libidinal energy occurs in some evangelical (and, in an oddly inconsistent way, in fundamentalist) worship services. The music often parallels that found in the secular culture; and there is an electric, emotional atmosphere reminiscent of early rock concerts. Acceptable modes of behavior (and body language) that involve touching and hugging, tap into an erotic primordial place in the unconscious. Some folks come away from such services "feelin' good" and laughing, but not knowing why. Others come away knowing that something within them was triggered that made them feel uncomfortable, also not knowing why. Jungian Robert

Moore has suggested that this energy is related to the
"Jesus as Lover" archetype held in the collective unconscious.[14] If the sensuality of one who is held up as
"Savior" has been relegated to the murky levels of the
collective unconscious, or pushed into the realms of the
shadow, the only way such libidinal energy can be
released is covertly. Surely this libidinal verve will not
be recognized by an institution that has separated itself
from such an acknowledgment.

Ulanov's second point has to do with the spiritual function of sexual polarity: "What is significant is
the role sexual polarity plays in helping us gain access
and relationship to the wider reaches of the psyche.
Sexual polarity introduces us to the mystery of otherness. The ego's meeting with the objective psyche is
symbolized by one sex meeting the other; this is the
spiritual function of sexual polarity."[15]

There is a difference here between polarization
and polarity. Today's culture mirrors the former, where
women and men place themselves in opposite, compet-
ing camps, with the women sneering at their "male
chauvinist pig" counterparts, who (with equal vigor) hurl
epithets of "castrating bitch" back at the women. The
polarity about which Ulanov speaks is one of psychological proportions, so that: "Sexuality in its symbolic
dimension has a spiritual function; it is the means and
signification of reunion with oneself, one's neighbor,
and God as the source of one's life."[16]

Here the dyadic interactions discussed above can
be clarified. If one cannot comprehend the psychically
symbolic, and errs in substituting the profane and
tangible for the spiritual and symbolic, the ensuing
consequences will be predictably painful. The key to
understanding human sexuality, then, is in understanding its spiritual purpose. Ulanov states:

One is simply oneself alone in polarization; in polarity one cannot be oneself,
except in and out of the love one shares.
It is the difference between parceling out
and being a part of. In polarity, one's
circumference is enlarged through a loss
of self in the other and the gaining of a
greater self. This greater self is not just
one or the other, nor just the two together, nor just a fusion of the two, nor just
the meeting of a soul with God. The
circumference encircles the two, the
fusion, and the relationship with God.[17]

The sensual aspects of the relationship between Mary
Magdalene and Jesus, and the spiritual quality of the
love they shared, can be understood in this way. The
realization of the "circumference" which "encircled the
two" is the manifestation of "the fusion," a fusion which
occurs when the risen Christ and the grieving Mary
Magdalene come face to face in the garden.

Mary Magdalene, in this encounter, and in the
vision related in the Gnostic *Gospel of Mary*, is empowered by the same Spirit of God which propelled the
dead Jesus upright, out of death, into transcendent
resurrection. She, who takes a risk that the male disciples shunned, is infused with a radiant Divine hope of
both chthonic and mysterious proportions. The transformation of a human Jesus into a divine Christ finds
its counterpart in Mary Magdalene, who can no longer
"cling to" her physical friend or mate. She must step
beyond that clinging to a place of autonomous spiritual
strength. She is then empowered to become the one
who is, indeed, the apostle to the apostles, the first
woman apostle. And she is the one, who in their time

of grief and despair, can "turn them toward the Good."
When the disciples rejected her account of her encounter with Christ (in the Gnostic vision) it was partly because they could not understand her aphoristic and feminine articulation of this vision.   She represented the feminine in such an unparalleled way; and, "The feminine is not interested in abstract theories and logical reasons.   Feminine wisdom comes out of the marrow of the bone, out of the suffering of experience--the fish that comes out of the gut, not the bird out of the head."[18]   In her encounters Mary Magdalene displayed the courage of one who trusts enough to open her heart and her body, even though, "opening the body can open a crevice in the heart that becomes an abyss containing the pain of a lifetime."[19]

Notes

1. Kahlil Gibran, *The Garden of the Prophet* (New York: Alred A. Knopf, 1982), 61.

2. John Shelby Spong, *Born of a Woman: A Bishop Rethinks the Birth of Jesus* (San Francisco: Harper San Francisco, 1992), 194.

3. Ibid.

4. Ibid., 191-92.

5. John Sanford, *Healing Body and Soul: The Meaning of Illness in the New Testament and in Psychotherapy* (Louisville: Westminster John Knox Press, 1992), 102.

6. John Calvin, *Institutes of the Christian Religion*, ed. John T. McNeill and trans. Ford Lewis Battles (Philadelphia: The Westminster Press, 1960), 35.

7. Ibid., 37.

8. Ibid., 43.

9. Ibid., 61-62.

10. Ibid., 38.

11. Ibid., 52.

12. My concern here is that I have explained only part of the complex, psychic dynamics which are part of this dyadic acting-out. The scope of this study does not allow for an adequate explanation of all those other shadow and archetypal pieces which comprise the whole. Jungian Linda Leonard has written two books which can be helpful in understanding the archetypal aspects of such acting out. They are: *The Wounded Woman: Healing the Father-Daughter Relationship* (Boston: Shambhala, 1982/85), and *On the Way to the Wedding*: Transforming the Love Relationship (Boston: Shambhala, 1986).

13. Ann Belford Ulanov, *The Feminine in Jungian Psychology and in Christian Theology* (Evanston, Ill.: Northwestern University Press, 1971), 26.

14. Robert Moore, "Healing the Masculine" (Lecture delivered at the C. G. Jung Institute in Chicago, 1991).

15. Ulanov, *The Feminine in Jungian Psychology and in Christian Theology*, 37.

16. Ibid., 14.

17. Ibid., 302.

18. Marion Woodman, *The Pregnant Virgin: A Process of Psychological Trans-formation* (Toronto: Inner City Books, 1985), 164.

19. Ibid.

9

Seeking a Transcendent Body/Spirit

"Sacred humanity is the spirit of divinity on earth. That humanity which stands amidst ruins clothing her nakedness in ragged garments, and shedding abundant tears upon her withered cheeks; calling upon her sons in a voice that fills the air with lament and mourning.

The sons that hear her not for the chanting of their battle hymns; who flee from her tears in the flashing of gleaming swords."

--Kahlil Gibran, *A Tear and a Smile*[1]

Introducing a feminine facet, or women's experience, into Christian theology is challenging to say the least, because it impinges upon old value systems which, as *habits of the mind*, have been held sacred for thousands of years. The collective majority still believes sexuality and spirituality are opposites. The chasm between a split body and soul swallows any attempt to incorporate a balance between the genders in the godhead.

Addressing God as Mother, or adding the Virgin

Mary to the Trinity, are (both) suggestions offered in recent times, but both may be too simplistic. The latter is not a solution at all, but only continues the sterile image of woman which has resulted from a projection of superior holiness, sinlessness, and sexlessness onto Mary, the mother of Jesus. Mary's way of receiving the Holy Spirit is one of human receptivity to a penetration by the divine. Yet, a one-sidedness has persisted, which cannot allow the Virgin Mary a sensuous nature. If women had been taught that their bodies were sacred, precious vessels as a part of this legacy, then it would have been a beautiful, soul-inspiring legacy, indeed. But, instead, the opposite connotation has been derived from it, and it has created great pain for many women.

The dialogue/argument over God as Mother, or God as Father, is littered with the fragmented skeletons of archetypal projections and unconscious needs. Do those who demand that God must always be Mother, and never male, indicate by that very demand an unconscious need to heal old wounding related to their familial, birth father? Is the primary impetus a negative father complex? To perceive God as Mother, who holds us in a warm and secure embrace, feeding us when we hunger, is to view God through the comforting memory of our personal and peculiar involvement with our own physical mother. But God is more than, greater than, this intimate knowing of a physical mother.

Does the opposite notion apply? Do those who insist that God is, and always has been, Father, and never female, indicate by their insistence an unconscious need to heal old wounding related to familial birth mother? Is the psychic influence a negative mother complex? The attributes of a loving, human father, one who represents security and stability, give us a perspective on a God whose characteristics include these positive masculine traits which we know experientially. But this God, whose being is ultimately and finally clothed in mystery, is not bound by these characteristics or their particularity.

In recent years it has become increasingly apparent that both of these gender related images fail for those whose experience of birth family has been one of (physical or sexual) abuse and gross mistreatment. God as Father, or God as Mother, then fails as a transforming image because the imagination is limited to negative remembrances of these two figures.

The God who, in the Old Testament, is clearly "He" in a Judaic sense of the word, the God image who was conceived by male priests in reaction to goddesses, who were clearly worshiped as "She," is transformed in the New Testament by the very nature of Jesus' birth. Jesus, the Son of God, is born from a human woman's body.

Out of that sacred birthing, women should have been lifted to a new awareness of their spiritual identities and to a transcendent understanding of their sexuality. But, the misogynistic emphasis of early Christian writings, leaders, and *habits of the mind,* has robbed generations of women of their sacred, spiritual inheritance. Their sexuality has been demeaned and their spirituality has been stunted, distorted, and almost negated by the patristic traditions of the faith.

The Old Testament God who lingers in "He-ness," stands like a stubborn warrior, blocking the threshold of the God who would be an embodiment of "Otherness" or even "She-ness." If we accept the literalistic Christians' (both theologians and laity who most often demand that God remain "He") view of the birth of Jesus, that is, his birth is derived from a union between the Holy Spirit and his mother, then the human/God who is Jesus is born not the "Son of Man," because no *man* was a participant in his conception.[2] The enfleshed God who is first named Son of Man in the Old Testament apocalyptic text of Daniel is born a *Son of Woman*!

A modern interpretation of Mark's reference to Jesus' birth cannot fail to note that this author said, "Is not this the carpenter, the Son of Mary and brother of James and Joses and Judas and Simon, and are not his sisters here with us?" [Mark 6:3 - NRSV] This first book among the Synoptic Gospels does not include a birth story (nor does the Gospel of John). But, neither is this first book among the Synoptic Gospels apologetic about "the Son of Mary." Mark's gospel does not mention Joseph, nor does this author make the mother of Jesus into a dehumanized, sexless creature who does not have other children.

Jesus is born the Son of Mary, and this Son of Woman is the one who breaks the old tradition of law, and rigidity, and linear notions of a God who, in reality, transcends the human imagination. Women continue their struggle to articulate a Son of Woman. As that articulation finds its voice, in their hearts, and minds, and inner soul places, women will no longer accept the old dogmas that parade as "truth." Women are looking for a vision, not a law; women are reaching for a mystery, not a dogmatic creed; women need to embrace an embodied spirit, not a *Book Of Order*. The institutional church needs to hear the voices of women; it needs to accept the images that arise from the emerging feminine consciousness, for they hold new awarenesses of ourselves and of our images of God.

A feminine image of the church as a sacred

vessel or holy womb "can house the gap between our God-images and God."[3] The key to understanding this gap is one of learning that the church "is not the place where the gap is overcome" because:

> Only God overcomes the gap, in bits and pieces, in individual souls, communally. The church can help us to ready ourselves for grace, help us to spy it, to take it when it comes, to use it. ... It is a matter of atmosphere, a scent, a spirit in the air, that tells quickly whether the clergy are wrestling with the same gap in themselves, struggling with the gap between God-images and what is revealed in Scripture and tradition and by what God may seem to be saying to us today.[4]

As mainline denominations try to determine ways to appeal to those who claim the church is no longer relevant, addressing this gap will become increasingly important. This gap is part of the underlying reason for rejecting the church as an institution. But if the church can recognize itself as a holy bridge, one which can create an environment of security and acceptance, while its people struggle with the gap, then the church as an institution can, itself, be reborn.

The transcendent needs a place of holiness in order to be released. It is impossible to regenerate the world's vision of the numinous or the transformative without sacred space. The church has historically been that sacred space, but it no longer holds that unique distinction. The soul cannot be reborn without sacred space, a place that is a container for the numinous. Many of those who have rejected the institutional church are adrift, without a place for renewal and rebirth. They must seek out a spirit-birthing place, a holy enclosure for sacred renewal and soul rebirthing.

A God image who goes beyond the rigidity of He-ness is critical to this soul rebirthing process; a God image that is receptive to the feminine is vital for this hallowed containment. We need to enlarge our visions of "divine image" and of "holy ground," so that the church can embody and encircle the souls of those who so desperately need such sacred containment. And these ones are all of us! When we learn that our humanity is holy, and our own being (in every facet of our living) is meant to be sacred, we will no longer search the mountaintops for holy places. We will know they lie beneath our feet in places we have ignored or perhaps even partially destroyed.

One popular, New Age trend for many women who have this genuine yearning has been a turning toward goddess worship. But to regressively slip into goddess worship as the ultimate solution is unwise. Ann Ulanov writes:

> Women turn to goddess images to reach something alive and feminine that is so missing or so eclipsed in our culture that the only way to find it again is to cast it upwards metaphorically as divinity. Ironically, however, these goddess images can be a way of killing off the feminine as well, reverting to a view of woman as simply an impersonal natural force. In goddess religion woman is female sex, woman is blood, woman is fertility, woman is milk. We thus skip over or obliterate 2,000 years of woman estab-

lished as an individual, a particular soul, a person. The symbolism and the pre-Oedipal psychological dynamics of goddess imagery lead to merger of self and instinct, self and other, self and deity. Fusion is not union and loss of self differs radically from offering God the self one is and has. Women do not want to be reduced to a force of nature. Women want to be themselves, each one as she is, different, individual, greeted and cherished for herself and with that treatment joined to the whole human species.[5]

Goddess worship is regressive, failing to give adequate credence to the inherited cultural changes that have both paradoxically, and effectively, provoked its current popularity. It is a form of instinctual femininity, not conscious femininity. Those who merely scoff at goddess worship, without understanding the basis for its very seductive attraction, fail to address the depth of psychic/spiritual pain in women who have turned to it.

When no female vision is part of our understanding of God, when no feminine entity is part of our Trinitarian belief, we may turn to goddess imagery, or we may search for an appropriate metaphor. Many women theologians have looked to metaphors to elucidate the ambiguity of the Trinity. One of those metaphors is music; and I employ it here to enlarge the concept of Mary Magdalene's legacy. My symbolic, metaphorical Trinity would encompass a trio of interactive entities in that God, as Godhead and First Among Equals, is the one who composes the lyrics and the melody; Jesus Christ, the Son, is the one who sings the words and plays the notes; and the Spirit is a Mag-

dalene Spirit, who *is* the music. The Magdalene Spirit
is a flowing receptive force that gives enduring, but
quickening, fire to the very core of the human soul.

However, going beyond metaphor would allow,
"the feminine character of the Spirit" to be recognized.
Going beyond metaphor would bring about the "restitu-
tion of femininity to the dignity of the image of God.
Only then will also actual masculinity be seen in its
original dignity, and this masculinity will no longer
appear with the distorting character of domination."[6]

The dominator model of thinking cannot survive
in a modern world from whose collective consciousness
the demand for new imagery is rapidly emerging. But,
in the present moment, I believe the unconscious domi-
nators sense this change and are extremely threatened
by it.

As I complete the work on this book, the news
services speak of twenty (or maybe even thirty) thousand women being raped in the war of control for what
was once the nation state of Yugoslavia. There is a
feature story on sexual harassment of little girls, children who ride school buses in Minnesota and Texas,
children who are only eight to eleven years old. And
the boys who call them "Slut" and threaten to rape
them are only a few years older. When school authorities are confronted with this information, they protest
that this cannot be sexual harassment, because none of
these children are old enough to *be* sexual. Oh yes, the
dominator, controller collective is very threatened; it is
evident in the chaos that we read about in the newspa-
pers and in the evening news we see on our televisions.

I am reminded of the pain and despair of a
friend who told me, almost a year after her ordination
for the Ministry of the Word and Sacrament in another
denomination, of a movement by the men who were

members of the deacon's board to rescind her ordination. They were angry that her ordination had been approved by the district level of the denomination, and they were determined to take that ordination away from her, if they could. I have not forgotten that, on the day when I was examined for ordination, another woman was also examined. After the action to ordain her had been approved, a group of men filed a protest, one which implied their unconscious protestations more than their verbal ones. In each case these protests emerged around issues related to control and maintaining a male power base.

We cannot receive God into our interiority until we have first emptied ourselves of concepts of power and control, ones which are centered on a distorted power principle. The patriarchy knows nothing of surrender, it is driven to control and define and limit the very being of a God who cannot be controlled or defined or limited, a God whose very "essence is incomprehensible." Healing in the institutional church can only come through an awareness of the vital, creative aspects of internal, soul/body wholeness. The Trinity cannot be envisioned in new ways by those who are split apart in their internal places, so that a duality of dominator, subordinant is their only focus of imagination. Healing will not come until we understand that the God of history, the God of now, cannot be locked within any boundary.

There is a sense in which the institutional church is like a collective anorexic, one who refuses to take in and assimilate the newly emerging substance which is life-giving, life-prolonging, life itself. The church, flying in its grandiose spiritual realm, refuses this substance, this energy of embodied feminine consciousness and of positive masculine consciousness, of soul rebirthing spirit. Instead of opening itself to receive this timeless energy, the church obsesses upon negative sexuality, seeing only naked genitalia. This obsessive focus is evident from the earliest writings of the Christian "fathers" to the present day. It is ever the same when modern church leaders debate the "acceptability" of women priests.

The historical tradition of church dogma is akin to an albatross around the neck. Its stench overwhelms the one who continues to carry its burdensome edicts. The church, like the society, has focused upon outward things to the exclusion of internal soul needs. Instead of listening to the voice of the Great and Holy Spirit who speaks from the belly, it has invested its energy and its imagination in outmoded, ethnocentric, and brain-level interpretations from the past.

The wholeness of God's reality can only come when we have emptied our collective understandings of those negatives which continue to cripple and smother creativity. When egocentric notions of control are surrendered, then the soul is emptied and opened to receive the numinosity of the Holy Spirit. The struggle to bring the purest essence of spirit to body is the struggle to bring balance to the Trinity. It is a struggle to overcome the negative heritage of Judaic Dualism and Neo-platonic thought held deeply in the collective unconscious.

The unfortunate inheritance of the church is one of disembodied spirit. Disembodied spirit is the source of rejection for many of those who have left the institutional church. Disembodied spirit believes it owns and speaks the only version of Truth for the institutional church. Disembodied spirit demands perfection that is clearly beyond our human capabilities. The musculature that is our very human substance is rejected by a disembodied spirit.

In fact, disembodied spirit calls forth rage in those who have had "good little girl/boy" projected upon them by their parents or church. When spirit is equated only with male/father, and God is equated only with Father, then mother church becomes the object for projections of the negative mother complex, and then the church itself can be rejected because of the devouring, smothering symbol it represents. An objectified mother can always be rejected.

The disembodied spirit believes itself to be suprahuman and superior, so superior that its inborn sexuality must be denied. The disembodied spirit, from its place of pseudo-superiority, believes itself incapable of an immoral act. The negative source of that denial is unveiled when it projects immorality onto others. The human body wants to be redeemed, but it cannot be redeemed in a church that is only a stagnant pool of theological sludge. The church has degenerated into the melancholy of stagnant, creedal imagery. It can only move to the dawn of new creativity when it takes the leap of faith that will bring it into ensouled embodiment.

Only an embodied spirit, holding the transcendence of a fresh new "image of God" within, can redeem the rejected substance of frail, imperfect humanity. The wholeness of body/spirit, in its totality, is God and the essence of God. The heart, soul, mind, body, belly, gut, and yes, even the poor misused and mistreated genitalia, every piece of the blood, and ligament, and spirit that is life, itself, must be embraced as part of God. For if any portion therein is rejected, then the totality is fragmented and God dies in this fragmentation.

The spirit does not easily accept the notion of

returning to its place in the body, anymore than the institutional church accepts the wisdom of a female entity in the Trinity. The spirit that is inflated by a collective still embracing Neo-platonic (and Jewish Dualistic) ideals wants to fly free, like a Peter Pan. It wants to hold itself apart in the dichotomous and distorted apocalyptic place of "light versus darkness." But the blinded doctrine of past tradition needs to give way for the birthing of new body/spirit. That body/spirit understands love and the giving of love, it understands that the human and God are inextricably connected, and it affirms that embodied connectedness.

The historical tradition that has taken Mary Magdalene's apostolic spirituality and set it apart, discounting its connection to her innate sensual energy, has reduced the wholeness of her being, and the being of subsequent womankind, to a sum total of twisted sexuality. The one-dimensional portrait we have of her is far from the reality of her vital woman's body/spirit, even as the one-dimensional model for all women is far from the reality of even one woman.

To reject Mary Magdalene is to reject the visceral, grounded aspects of being in the body and in the soul. It is a rejection of all our inherent human limitations and frailties. The male-dominated church has killed the Mary Magdalene spirit, and it can only be integrated by women today when it is resurrected.

Mary Magdalene (even with an image of "fallen sinful woman) is grounded in her inheritance of human sexuality. In that grounding she can bring a new voice of lyrical praise which not only frees her transcendent energy, but rescues the shadow of Jesus Christ. The projection which has disfigured and crippled Mary Magdalene's spirituality has, in its opposite extreme, given the human Jesus an inauthentic, asexual image.

The denial of Jesus' full humanity, and thus the denial of Jesus' shadow, is at the heart of the split between spirit and body. The patriarchal rejection of women clergy evolves out of this inheritance of a disembodied spirit, out of the denial of shadow. The scapegoated one is represented by the body and sexuality and all that has historically been declared "unclean." As long as the body is denigrated to a place of imperfection, while the spirit is perceived as perfect, and thus superior, then the contra-sexual elements of the God image cannot be realized within the human soul.

Mary Magdalene is the symbolic scapegoat; she has been assigned the duty of carrying the burden of the dark, shadow side of Jesus. A church who only allows its Savior to embody the light of perfection has pushed his scapegoated loved one into the depths of theological purgatory. Long denied, Jesus' shadow lies within the whimpering womb of a woman who does not need to bring it to birth. The transcendence of Jesus' resurrection frees his human shadow; Mary Magdalene no longer needs to be burdened with it.

Mary Magdalene, and her legacy, can then become the symbolic container for Trinitarian change. While the available scripture, both accepted canon and Gnostic works, leave Mary Magdalene devoid of human offspring, she has been pregnant for two thousand years with the God-music of human female spirituality. She carries it within herself, revealing the inexplicable to Christ's disciples. Her being is penetrated by, blossoms with, and carries in eternal containment, the God-music needed for sexual/spiritual healing. That God-music is capable of healing the anger held in the bodies and bulging in the souls of countless women, clergy and laity alike. It can soothe and heal the wounds left by those whose need for power and control have kept the

Godhead exclusively male. It can be transformed into eloquent and poetic prayers of new imagery of a God being, an enlarged vision of Godness.

Mary Magdalene embodies the unlived recognition of the holy which our culture has sublimated into an unhealthy acting out in the body, thus contaminating and soiling even the sacred. With a sacred penetration of God-music, of Magdalene Spirit, a profound linking of two archetypal opposites can occur, so that wisdom is no longer set apart from a beguiling primordial energy. Then spirituality is not separated from sexuality; the flesh and the spirit are reunited, and the woundedness we have inherited from Jewish Dualism and Greek philosophy can be healed.

So Mary Magdalene offers her God-music. She holds it out to us, who have felt it swelling in the belly, springing from the heart, and rushing from our souls. The muted voice of her sacred song is bursting with the very nature of her unfinished symphony, breaking forth as a new voice for a church stumbling and flailing about in its confusion over imagery. Yet, to understand her song is to understand that it was, and is, and always will be unfinished and incomplete. The embodiment of the true feminine is always incomplete, always unfinished, and yet it lacks nothing. To know her song is to know that it lies in that place where abstract theory cannot go. To hear her music is to know that its questions must remain unanswered, for they are floating upon a melody that stands in the chasm between the revealed nature of God and the impenetrable mysterion. And Mary Magdalene weeps for those who have needed her sensual embodied spirituality, tears from which pour her God-music, tears that drop like raindrops into the lake of the mysterion.

Notes

1. Kahlil Gibran, *A Tear and a Smile*, trans. H. M. Nahmad (New York: Alfred A. Knopf, 1950), 191.

2. Here I do not intend for the reader to assume I believe in a literal interpretation of the "virgin" birth. I do not. The virgin birth, like much of the dogmatic tradition of the church, is based upon an apologetic insistence that the mother of Jesus, the Son of God, must be without sexuality. To rob her of her sexuality is to rob her of her innate humanity. It was part of the early Christian apologetic need to explain the birth of Jesus. A book which explores this subject is Jane Schaberg's *The Illegitimacy of Jesus: A Feminist Interpretation of the Infancy Narratives* (New York: Crossroad; A Meyer-Stone Book, 1990).

3. Ann Belford Ulanov, *The Wisdom of the Psyche* (Cambridge: Cowley Publications, 1988), 130.

4. Ibid.

5. Ibid., 87.

6. Elisabeth Moltmann-Wendel and Jürgen Moltmann, *Humanity in God* (New York: The Pilgrim Press, 1983), 103.

10

Reflections Upon the Now

"You are my brother and we are the children of one universal holy spirit. You are my likeness, for we are prisoners of two bodies formed of one clay. ...
    Say of me what you will and the morrow will judge you, and your words shall be a witness before its judging and a testimony before its justice."
                        --Kahlil Gibran, *A Tear and a Smile*[1]

Reflections upon the now are almost always tinged with the colors of, and shaped by, the ordinary, the mundane, and the gut-wrenchings of the past. I am a woman born into a family of five siblings. Being born the first daughter after three sons was remarkable only in that my birthing was one of rejection by the patriarch personified in my father. When my mother gave birth to me, in the front room of that old Virginia farmhouse where we all grew to adulthood, my father refused to come into the room, to speak to my mother, or to look at me, for three days.

He had wanted another son, and when he was presented with a daughter, he pouted for three days. (Of course, all this occurred more than fifty years ago. It was a time when men were unaware that their sperm carried the gender-determining factor.)   Only after a sound tongue-lashing by the old doctor who had overseen this birthing, did my father, in shame, then enter the room, greet my mother, and touch me for the first time.   I understand, in the most visceral way, the meaning of rejection because of my gender.

My mother, herself "a daughter of the patriarchy,"[2] was a woman who grieved for much of her adult lifetime.   That grief was centered upon her knowing that she had chosen a life of wifehood, when her intellect, talents, and skills, wanted and needed a larger arena for their creative outbursting.   By the time she reached my age, she already believed herself to be an old woman, and when she died twenty-odd years later, she was old beyond her years and bitter with it.   Her faith, while spoken with certainty and sureness, was scarcely evident as she made her way from sickbed to hospital bed, only to return and languish upon our sofa. That bodily sickness, with the soul wounding it manifested, and her unrewarded intellect, gave birth to physiological symptoms carved on the back of psychic pain.   Those are the pieces of my mother's self which hang from cobwebs of my memories of her.

Her mother before her had been a woman of Bible-clutching faith, whose ultimate and only solace came from pouring over the pages of her old, frayed King James Bible.   She carried it with her when she came to visit; she read aloud to me from it, even as my mother read aloud from this same English version while we finished our breakfasts in the morning.   These were women of good and faithful Christian belief, and yet neither one of them ever had an opportunity to live to her fullest potential. They, like countless others, were the daughters and granddaughters of a social system that prohibited such fullness of living. It was a social system known as patriarchy.

My father was a man who was the only son of a powerful woman, a woman who held his psyche tightly in check all the years she lived. Even though he had rebelled against this strong mother, he continued to dance the steps that she set, like a marionette on the strings manipulated by her forceful puppeteer hands. His ways of being with his children and his wife were grounded in his unconscious belief that males were superior. He had to believe this; he needed to believe this. With a father who had died before his birth, it was the only way he could absolve himself of his symbiotic dependency upon a tyrannical mother. She was, in her own way, the embodiment of the patriarchy. Emulating male behavior patterns of power, she exercised despotic control over her family.

My father, like his mother, became a tyrant. He held tightly to the patriarchal reigns of power in his household, believing that he could dictate even the thought processes of his children and his wife. Our knowing of ourselves was filtered through the assumptions cast upon us from a powerfully vocal father. The children in his family grew up dreading his anger and its accompanying vicious temper tantrums. Rage was one of the manipulating tools he used to force his ways of being upon his family.

My mother, in reaction, became a woman who raged at times and who dissolved into the wretchedness of body illness at others. Her understanding of her potential options, and of the way her life was to be played out, finally melded with, and acquiesced to, my father's exercise of power over her and upon her children. Theirs was the joint legacy of the patriarchy. Theirs was the typical, and oh-so-painful living out of such dominant, subordinate belief. Theirs was the sadness of long generations who had lived their whole lives in emptiness because of such a stratified social system.

To remember that sadness, and the void at the center of such lives, is a sacred task. In my remembering of such despair, I myself, strive to live fuller and richer days. In that remembering I have learned to trust the very being of myself and of myself in relation to my divine Creator. For in such remembering, and in the telling of it, I believe others are brought to healing, and perhaps even those who died without hope for a new day, or a new way of thinking, will somehow be healed too.

In (Judaic) Kabbalistic thought there is a fascinating and wonderful understanding of that moment in time when God (as an identifiable entity) becomes God; it is that time when God steps out of a place of concealment and is "made manifest." That moment comes when God becomes the creator. When God creates, then God, as a Godself, is made known through this very act of creating. Only in creating is God revealed. The God who creates the universe *ex nihilo* (out of nothing) comes forth out of this same mysterious place.[3] But then, even the notion of *ex nihilo* is called into question, for God's act of creation is not a solitary act of aloneness. To whom is the God in the canonical statement "Let us make humankind in our image," speaking? This God/head does not stand alone.

I believe that the flowing, receptive essence of God, the wonderful Shekhinah, stood there with this

God, and in that magnificent moment--that which was most secret, even the most sacred secret, was revealed when God and humans were brought together as creator and created. Then God was identifiable, even as the human became a *nephesh*, "a living being." Then the human and the God, with breath and spirit and lives intermingled, launched themselves into a potentiality for noble living or for evil existence.

Many other cultures have similar understandings of God and human interdependent creativity. As an example, the old ones of the Inuit tribe "say that the breath of a god and the breath of a human, when commingled, cause a person to create an intense and holy poetry."[4] These, indeed, are things the soul knows, but the mind, from its rational, proof-demanding constructs, resists. The Kabbalistic concept is not one most mainline Jews would embrace, it comes out of a mystical tradition. A soul-level knowing of God is not one that mainline Christians embrace, it is set aside because it stands too far off the periphery of dogmatic understandings.

I believe that God must be re-imagined in the present day. I believe that God's redemption, and surely the church's salvation, depends upon such creative imagination. I am a "Reformed" Christian, even as the Presbyterian Church, U.S.A. is a reformed denomination. The church that holds up a faith belief of "reformed, always reforming," must be willing to live that articulated belief. If it does not, it cannot blame others for its demise.

Part of our living, part of our human, spiritual journey is shared by every other human being on the face of the earth. While I do not know with great clarity the journey of many others, I do have a knowing of my own journey, and this book is inauthentic without telling of that knowing as honestly as I can. I am a cradle Presbyterian, born into this branch of the Protestant tradition, and through all else, fiercely loyal to it.

What I have revealed about my church is, in my belief, a sacred secret. I suspect it will be a sacred secret that is denied by the hierarchy (who claim to uphold denominational egalitarian standards), excoriated for its bias, and dismissed, perhaps as the ravings of one who represents something close to the lunatic fringe! And yet, my personal journey through the care process of the Presbyterian Church, U.S.A. "thrust" me closer to a contemplation of suicide than any other experience of my lifetime. In the depths of those days, and weeks, and months of abject grief, I knew that I could either collapse into my own shadow, allow it to consume me, and in fact, step into the fatal maw of suicide. Or I could hang on for dear life, literally, and when my grief was abated, I could write about this experience from the place of one who had walked through "the valley of the shadow of death."

I am not a youngster, whose life experience has been so minuscule, that this negative one should overshadow all others. I have stood by my (now deceased) husband's hospital bed for a long and terrible thirty-eight days. I have waited during those days and nights in the waiting room of an intensive care unit. I have watched as he fought and hung on to life and lived for four more years. I have then grieved for the death of this man, a man with a brilliant mind, and yet a soul so wounded that he could not lift himself up and confront the shadow aspects of that wounding. I have stood by the hospital beds of my father and my mother and watched as their faces took on that "mask of death," and they drifted away into that unknown place that is death. And, I have grieved for a baby that came too soon, who could not live, who did not live.

My knowing of grief is not so sparse that I have been consumed by this one experience of grief. But, this particular experience of grief is one which needs to be articulated in such a way as to call attention to it. This experience of grief is one that I know has been shared by others, usually women. My knowing of my God surely was reshaped by my *care process*.

I was forced to set aside any idealistic notions of being truly cared for, as I walked the hazardous trek that was my candidacy journey. I was forced to set aside my hopes for a blessing during this process. I had believed that this journey would incorporate the blessings which are Biblical in character, and one would assume, implicit to a *care process*. Instead I was forced to recognize that my journey under care was one that carried an implicit curse, one derived from a *habit of the mind of male superiority* and thus a negative, archetypal core. While I cannot know the experience of others who have embarked upon this spiritual exodus, I do not believe that mine was so singular, or so unusual, that others cannot identify with it. It is my belief that, on the contrary, many women clergy--Presbyterian and other denominational affiliates, have had parallel experiences, even ones which would make mine pale by comparison. I believe these women have quietly acquiesced to the powers of their respective church hierarchies, and have held their anger inside, sometimes concealing its depth and breadth even from themselves. But, if the church is ever going to function from a healthy place, and not a co-dependent, dysfunctional one, these kinds of mistreatments must be ended--and the truth about them must be told.

And so I have written of my own personal experience, even as I have written of the lost legacy of Mary Magdalene. There may be those who will sense some kind of parallel, and suggest that I have over-identified with this woman whose story is so brief, and yet so much a part of my understanding of my faith. There may even be a bit of truth in such a suggestion; a *daughter of the patriarchy* is rarely without wounding related to authentic and healthy understandings of both her sexuality and her spirituality. Yet, I contend that the Magdalene projection continues today; it continues each time a woman is mistreated on her journey toward ordination. There may be others who will be quick to condemn my intuitive reading of the text, and of my interpretation of it through that same modality. All this I recognize, but yet . . .

I believe that God is more real and more accessible when intuitive, belly-level honesty is a vital part of knowing God. As long as the church continues to poke its collective, ostrich-like head into the sands of past tradition, all the while claiming that tradition as the only form of Truth, then it will die the death that has been pronounced upon it for decades. It will not live if it continues to be the very representation of so much that is superstitious, and ignorant, and plainly at odds with contemporary human reality.

When bright, well-educated people, like my daughter, and numerous friends who are dear to me, cannot tolerate the anachronistic understandings through which the church defines itself, it is no longer a viable institution for transformation. My daughter looks me in the eye and, with a candor that holds honesty at its very core, declares that she is "not Christian." She has rejected that heritage, because that heritage is besmirched with lies, which are covered over with denial, in order to protect tradition. Out of her candor has come much of my courage, courage to address the ills of a church, that even now, I love dearly.

God cannot be realized with lively vigor as long as this God is encompassed round about by a dishonest, fearful tradition, because "a tradition without intelligence is not worth having"[5] It is my hope that others, both women and men, who have had experiences not dissimilar from mine will find pieces of themselves within these pages. It is my hope that those who live by the rule that declares, "Do not remove the ancient landmark that your ancestors set up,"[6] will open their hearts to some small part of what I have written. For as long as "the dead govern the living,"[7] we are carrying within ourselves, in the very deep places of our souls, a deathness which will not allow new life to spring forth. It is my hope and prayer that those who have walked away from the churches of their ancestors, and a belief in a living God, will find a fragment, a knowing, of a new God within these pages.

When I was a child in the first grade, my parents, recognizing my innate musical ability, sent me off to take piano lessons. I was an abysmal failure at this new experience. Only in retrospect do I understand why. Music is a vital part of my life, and yet, I cannot take something which I receive and feel and understand at a chthonic level and transfer it to a cognitive place of precision and linear knowing. I adore music. I adore it from a soul-level place of purity. I still cannot read one note, but I love to sing, and singing has always been one of my finest pleasures.

I am thrilled by the resounding chords of a Tschaikowsky symphony. The lilting, yet dynamic, strains of Liszt never fail to cheer me. The soothing waltzes of Strauss will always remind me of Vienna and of hearing Strauss' music played there. I never fail to be amazed at the genius of Mozart. Even the ponderous, somber tones of Wagner suit some of my moods. I have sung great works by Bach, Handel, and Haydn. And yet, I cannot read one note of music; my knowing of music comes from a core of my being that is true and clear and "precise." I can memorize a piece of music and years later recall each note with precision, but it is a precision born out of the deepest, truly female part of myself. It is not a precision dependent upon the notes, or the time-signature, or any other aspect that is related to a cognitive knowing of the music. It comes out of the belly; it is derived from the gut.

It is my belief that the greatest knowing of God comes from this same deep, chthonic place. The days of our living are meant to be undergirded by a melody emanating from a God-place within us. I believe that too many people, both women and men, have been cut off from that God-music within themselves. I believe that many factors have contributed to this severing of the soul from the uppermost levels of cognitive understanding. Beginning with the Enlightenment, and culminating in a scientific, technological age of information, the human soul has been pushed to a place of collective misunderstanding. But, the God-music has not gone away in despair.

The God-music is still there. It shines in the face of every child under the age of three who has not been socialized into covering their authenticity with the persona mask. It is written upon the countenance of one who slips back and forth across the borders between life and death. It floats in the air of every autumn day, along with the brightly colored leaves. We desperately need to recapture our God-music, our souls need to be embraced and lifted out of intellectual mire. I believe our very lives depend upon it.

Notes

1. Kahlil Gibran, *A Tear and a Smile*, trans. H. M. Nahmad (New York: Alfred A. Knopf, 1950), 192-93.
2. This term is used in Marion Woodman's *Leaving My Father's House: A Journey to Conscious Femininity*, (Boston: Shambhala Publications, 1993), 352.
3. Gershom Scholem, *Kabbalah* (New York: Dorset Press, 1987), 90-110.
4. Mary Uukulat, quoted by Clarissa Pinkola Estes, Ph.D., in *Women Who Run With The Wolves: Myths and Stories of the Wild Woman Archetype* (New York: Ballantine Books, 1992), 291.
5. T. S. Eliot, "After Strange Gods," from Rhoda Thomas Tripp's *The International Thesaurus of Quotations* (New York: Harper and Row Publishers, 1970), 645.
6. Proverbs 22:28, *The New Revised Standard Version of the Holy Bible* (Nashville: Cokesbury, 1990), 918.
7. Auguste Comte, *Catechisme positiviste*, from Rhoda Thomas Tripp's *The International Thesaurus of Quotations* (New York: Harper and Row Publishers, 1970), 645.

Appendix A

Each student who graduated from the Master of Divinity program (at seminary) was required to complete a "Statement of Faith." This Statement of Faith included each individual's articulation of their view of God, as well as a specific statement addressing a contemporary sociological phenomenon or dynamic which demands the response of the institutional church.

While these statements were intended to reflect the authentic belief of the writer, there was an understanding that they would also reflect the parameters of the faith as it is perceived by the institutional church, in my case, the Presbyterian Church, U.S.A. This statement was then defended in an oral examination before a team of faculty members.

Many of the students who graduated with me told of this encounter with painful recollections; they were required to rewrite their statements in order to meet the demands of this or that professor. In the end, their statements bore little resemblance to their original. Instead, they represented the perspective of those professors before whom they had defended their statements.

I was extremely fortunate in the team of faculty with whom I worked. The following statement is the original as it was presented to my team of faculty. The two men who examined me on this statement did not require that one word be changed. Somehow it was as if the Spirit flowed naturally and with ease between these two men and myself. They seemed to intuitively know that I was skating on very thin psychic ice. Their affirmation at that time was exactly what I needed. In my soul, it ranks as one of the most life-giving moments in my seminary journey.

* * * * * * * * * *

PERSONAL STATEMENT OF FAITH

Completed November 1990

I believe in God, the Author of Creation, in Jesus, the Christ, the Son, and in the Holy Spirit. While my God has been active in the history of humanity, this God cannot be limited by human expectations or human parameters. God stands outside the ability of humans who attempt to describe the being or the nature of God. While many creedal statements regarding God are admirable attempts to encompass the being or nature of God, all human descriptions fall short of a God who cannot be described in our language, whatever that language may be. We paint pictures from the eyes of our imaginations, we write creeds which paint word pictures, and we press for an understanding in our liturgies; all are inadequate. I cannot describe the larger than human aspects of this God, who nevertheless is and has been powerfully interactive in human history.

While I believe God cannot be bound by human limitations I do not mean to imply that God is distant and/or unapproachable. God is, on the contrary, very near. God stands side by side with me as I recall the images from the Old Testament. Thus, this God who is my God is for me a Rock, a Holy and Divine Parent who cradles me when I am hurting, and feeds me when I hunger, and under whose wings I may shelter myself in times of need. This God is not limited to the anthropomorphic notions of gender specificity. God is greater and more than either a God, as Father, or God, as Mother. Even to use both labels often pushes God into stereotypical assumptions, creating a dichotomous split which narrows and confines that which cannot be viewed from such a small perspective.

I believe the most intimate connection I have with God came in the first moment of life. In that moment I became the inheritor of "the image of God," so that God, as Creator, becomes real for me. I believe I was graciously endowed with God-given breath, but breath which is more than breath, one that is the progeny of the historic Hebrew *nephesh*. With this *nephesh* God has quickened my being and made it sacred, so that I am one spirit/one body, undivided before God. I am blessed by this way in which God imprints a divine "image" upon me, and in that blessing know that it establishes the holy obligation for the way in which I interact with all others. All other humans have been endowed with this same "image" and with this same divine breath of "living being." I must, then, honor the created image of God in my interactions with others, because when I remember that they bear this same image, I cannot treat them without honor and respect.

I believe that Jesus, the Son of God, was born into history as a Jew in Nazareth. Jesus experienced his humanity in every sense of the word, feeling the pangs of being pushed into the world through birth. His human experience, in all its dimensions, gives meaning to mine. His joy lifts my joy to a different level, his sorrow makes mine more understandable, his acceptance of others provokes me to examine my ability to do likewise. His despair pushes me to challenge my own despair and to probe for its meaning, his anger makes mine seem less odious, and his life style forces me to weigh my priorities on a continuing basis.

The hideous aspects of Jesus' death seem to reflect the remarkable face of my moments of rejection of God, even as the transcendence of his resurrection gives light and life to my moments of acceptance. The contrast between the two is so pronounced; yet when I am honest, I know that I could have stood in both crowds. I could have been overcome with the joy and pure exhilaration of that moment when Jesus came riding into the city; I would have lifted my arms and shouted with glee, proclaiming him the Messiah. And only a few days later, I could have stood among the throngs of those who screamed "Crucify Him!" My frailty is a human thing; my ultimate hope is in that which is divine. I have no illusions about my fallibilities, but because Jesus lived his life in human form, I am assured that my humanity will be understood, even in its worst moments. This does not relieve me of living my life in a responsible manner, or translate into an esoteric withdrawal from human interaction. Instead, Jesus is the means whereby I measure my living. I cannot achieve the consciousness which he exhibited, but I can strive to emulate the patterns of his living.

The Holy Spirit is a powerful, divine catalyst for change in my living and in my understanding of both God and humanity. The Holy Spirit is not some abstract entity, or a gender related personification, but an energy felt at the most visceral levels of my being. When the voice of God comes to wake me from sleep, the Holy Spirit carries the message, forcing me to rouse myself and pay attention. If God composes the lyrics and the melody, and Jesus, the Christ and the Son, sings the words and plays the notes, then the Holy Spirit *is* the music.

The Holy Spirit is the flowing, receptive force which gives enduring, quickening fire to my spirit, to the very core of my being. It is the container from which the *nephesh* of my being was sprung, and it is the divine energy which pushes me beyond old, tired understandings of God, and of myself. The Holy Spirit infuses my being with a transcendent quality, a quality not easily framed in a verbal statement. It is an experience which flows out of the belly, not out of the head. The Holy Spirit moves in the "marrow of the bones," not through a linear formulation of the mind. The Holy Spirit gives texture, and unlimited facets, and glowing color to the otherwise flat dimensions of my existence. The Holy Spirit embodies both the chthonic and the mysterious; opening my heart and empowering my living.

The Bible is the authoritative source of my understanding of this trinitarian God. Beyond this source I have come to my understanding of God and myself through an education which encompasses both lived experience and the works of scholars and theologians who have struggled to define God and the manifestations of God. My Christianity does not stand outside the very strong influence of Judaism. I worship the God of the Old Testament, even as I embrace the Jesus of the New Testament. Jesus was a Jew, who taught from a Jewish perspective, and those teachings articulate my understanding of Christian living. Jesus cannot be separated from the prophetic understandings of the Old Testament, and as he embodies the fulfillment of those prophecies, he enlarges my vision of God to encompass the totality of the Scriptures, even as he enlarges my understandings of the person of God.

The Scripture of the Bible does not have to be scientifically and historically accurate, or without error, for me to accept it as the definitive authority through which my God is apprehensible. I believe those who wrote the Bible were touched by the Holy Spirit in such a way as to write what was written. If some of what was written is not "perfect," it reassures me that my imperfection can be brought before the same God who is articulated in this canon. I can read this text with the sure and certain knowing that God will give me the tools for understanding as much of the text as I am meant to understand. And if I err in my interpretation of that text, God is larger than my human failure to understand, and will temper the impact of my understanding, usually with compelling questions from another, whose ability to understand is greater than mine. Whenever I come to the text, I do so with no little trepidation; my human experience is so small, compared to the largeness of the message. But, God knows the extent and the limitations of my experience, and the grace of God is inherent in the risk I take, each time I dare interpret a small piece of the greater whole which is the Scripture. Without this grace to undergird my efforts, I would not have the courage to open this Book in the first place.

My ministry evolves out of that grace and my assurance of its transforming pattern in my life. I do not come to the ministry without argument; like Jonah, and various and sundry others, I have long protested. I come to the ministry out of a past history of authoritarian preachers, and Sunday school teachers, and family members who made bald pronouncements about a judgmental God whose overweening wrath was kindled at every angle.

There was precious little of warmth, or love, or compassion in such a God; the ghost-like apparition of a terrible, tyrant God hovered over my childhood understandings, stifling and stultifying the glorious aspects, the beautiful imagery, the uplifting qualities. As an adult, I have wrestled with those old images of God and come to a place of reconciliation with a God who offers both compassion and grace, but demands responsible living in return. My ministry, then, is one which I hope will articulate the balance between the two, so that I will espouse neither a God who is namby-pamby, nor overwhelming in tyrannical judgment.

I bring skills honed in the business arena to my ministry. I come to the very necessary tasks of administration with a strong ability to manage those tasks. I am grateful for this past work experience, because I believe it will be an enabling factor in the work I must do as a minister. I come to the ministry with experience as a lay preacher and as a staff financial officer for my presbytery. This experience, too, will enhance my ability to do the work of parish ministry. I want to be a good preacher, and a good teacher. I enjoy studying and preparation; that part of me which is quite introverted is easily immersed in the text or a commentary on the text. From this disciplined perspective on study, I hope to bring informed, thoughtful sermons and Christian Education material to others.

My ministry will take its place within the collective of those who are both the people of God and members of the Presbyterian denomination. I come from the midst of this collective and it has been the seedbed for my faith. While I have been fortunate enough to widen the dimensions of my faith through a wide variety of ecumenical experience, my loyalty to the Presbyterian denomination is strong. I believe in the egalitarian themes of Presbyterian polity and the mutuality of ministry which is shared by clergy and laity, alike. I have been an active participant in the life of this denomination as part of the laity; I look forward to a continuing ministry as a part of the clergy. My ability to minister is enlarged and blessed by the participation of all those others who share in it, I do not stand apart from them, or in authority over them, but walk with them as we learn with and from each other. The threads of our commonality bind us together for this shared undertaking; we do not stand or walk alone.

The critical ethical issue of our time which most troubles me has to do with the Christian church's harsh stance on homosexuality and lesbianism. In a short article, dated July 9, 1990, Time Magazine reported that "Reform Judaism last week became the first major U.S. religious body to adopt a national policy that sanctions homosexual behavior." The article notes that the statement approved by Reformed rabbis reads, "All

Jews are religiously equal regardless of their sexual orientation."[1] I believe the Christian church has, once again, been led by Judaism and it is my hope that very soon those of us who call ourselves "Christian," will offer the same gracious understanding to "all Christians."

I stand among the ranks of those who are viewed as "normal" and weep for those who have been labeled "deviant." I stand mute before those who are my friends, who are part of the gay community, and hope my friendship reflects the grace I, myself, need to be offered. What words can I say when acid pronouncements of accusation and degradation and condemnation are hurled by the very institution I am training to serve. I only know that *all* humans are created in the "image of God." For me this means all, and not some elite group of superior people who are endowed with so-called normal sexual orientation. If I dare to pass judgment on another, my slate had better be extraordinarily clean. My slate is not so clean nor sweet, and never has been. So, out of my own place of fragility and flawed mortality, I am in no position to condemn others.

Last year, in relation to the work I was doing in a nearby metropolitan hospital, I had the rare and wonderful opportunity to be befriended by a woman who is a lesbian. Very early in our C.P.E. (clinical pastoral education) experience together, she came to me and told me she wanted to talk. That evening we sat together in the chaplaincy office on the sixth floor of that hospital, and through tears and laughter she told me she was gay. I felt unbelievably honored and blessed by the trust she exhibited in telling me, a stranger, that she was gay. I am old enough to be this woman's mother; my own daughter is five years older than she. I somehow played the role of a surrogate mother to her, because she has not and probably will never tell her own mother that she is gay. But she told me, and in doing so, she took an enormous risk. She came and offered this critical secret about herself, and in the doing of it, she affirmed my ministry for me. In that moment, she extended a heartfelt trust that went beyond ordinary bounds; it was a moment in which we were both uplifted and affirmed as God's good creation, as women together.

It has been a little over a year since she was bold enough to tell me about herself. In that time I have met the young woman with whom she has a strong, loving relationship. They have welcomed me into their close-knit circle of friends, never once rejecting me because I am not "like" them. They have personified Christian love, trust, and compassion in their acceptance of one who is not part of their life style. I have become a sort of den mother to them, and their group of young lesbian friends, many of whom are students at the Baptist seminary. The human face of one who is gay, and also one's friend, transcends timeworn, stereotypical notions about lesbianism.

The dying face of one who has AIDS cannot be condemned. The sweat-drenched countenance of the patients whom I encountered at the hospital does not make me believe that AIDS is some sort of divine judgment visited upon those who are ultimately evil. Those patients, and their suffering mothers and sisters and brothers, were like a new manifestation of Job's horror, set in a modern hospital room. When clergy come to make pronouncements like Job's so-called "friends," and are equally as discomforting, then the clergy and all others need to examine the authority whereby those pronouncements are made. Oh, I know the old arguments about Paul's exhortations to the Romans are trotted out as the "Biblical authority" for such condemnations. But, I believe that Paul's edicts on this subject reflect an ethnocentric and egocentric stance which is quite applicable in a modern arena, a stance which is unacceptable for me. I do not believe that I am in a position to "cast the first stone." I only know I need to offer the respect and honor of the "image of God" to all other human creatures. How can I contaminate their embodiment of the essence of the Holy Spirit by uttering judgment against them? I am not in a position to make such judgments about them. I do not claim to be above such judgment making or to living a noble life. I only know that when I project my own inadequacy and my own darkness onto another, it always comes back to haunt me. Ultimately, there is only and always the grace, God's grace, and it is in living in that grace that hope abounds, and the spirit flies free of tainted accusations and judgments.

Note

1. Richard N. Ostling, "Gay Rabbis: Toppling An Ancient Tradition," *Time*, July 9, 1990, 62.

Appendix B

The *Book of Order* of the Presbyterian Church, U.S.A., also requires that each candidate for the Ministry of the Word and Sacrament write a succinct Statement of Faith (i.e., one single spaced type-written page) and defend it in an oral examination before their oversight committee. This Statement of Faith is also defended on the floor of the presbytery which examines the candidate for ordination. This statement is essentially a shortened version of the previous statement, with some interesting changes. I had not included the sacraments which are honored in the Presbyterian church in my first statement. It was surprising to me that the faculty team did not require a rewrite for that reason alone. But, instead, they pointed out that the sacraments were not mentioned, while affirming the statement itself as sound. I was reminded that I should put them into the statement going to presbytery, and most readers can tell that they were added later.

The reader will notice where cautious changes have been made to accommodate those in the denomination who will look for such language as *inerrant* regarding the Bible. While, at no time do I write that I believe in the "inerrancy of the text," I am careful not to include the same statements that were received and honored by my seminary faculty team. In my examination with them, I was warned that I should take great care about this specific subject, because of the conservative backlash within the denomination. Their advice was, indeed, good advice. When I was examined by my committee of care, this was the area upon which the pastor (who was most opposed to me) focused.

* * * * * * * * * *

PERSONAL STATEMENT OF FAITH

Completed January 1991

I believe in God, the Author of Creation; in Jesus, the Son and Redeemer; and in the Holy Spirit. While God has been active in the history of humanity, this God cannot be limited by human expectations or human boundaries. Even though the Eternal God is larger than human description, God is neither distant, nor unapproachable. My God is the God of the Old Testament who is a Rock of strength when I am weak, and a shelter when I am weary. My God is the God of the New Testament, whose power and compassion were closely attuned to the work of a human Jesus, the Son.

One of the intimate connections I have with God comes through my imprinted image. Because I am created in the "image of God," I know that all other humans carry this divine image too. That shared blessing endows me with the holy obligation to treat all others with the honor and respect implied by the "image of God."

I believe that Jesus, the Son of God, was born into history as a Jew in Nazareth. Jesus experienced his humanity in every sense of the word, being born with the same birth pangs as all humans. His human experience, in all its dimensions, gives meaning to mine. His joy lifts my joy to a different level, his sorrow makes mine more understandable, his acceptance of others provokes me to examine my ability to do likewise. His despair pushes me to challenge my own despair, his anger makes mine less odious, and his life style forces me to weigh my priorities on a continuing basis. Jesus is the means whereby I then measure my living; the Sacrament of Baptism is the way in which I celebrate Jesus' cleansing heritage.

The death and resurrection of Jesus are the means whereby I am given the ultimate hope of that same resurrection. Because Jesus, the Christ, left an empty tomb behind, he lifted my humanity to a place of redemption. The unknown pieces of death take on a different color and texture with this atonement, and I am given a hope that is larger than my human ability to understand, even as it is the hope in which I ultimately trust. The mystery of death is forever imprinted with the blood of a dying Christ. Jesus, the Christ, is the means whereby I then measure my dying; the Sacrament of the Lord's Supper is the ritual which calls me to remember Christ's atonement.

The Holy Spirit is a powerful, divine catalyst for change in my life and in my understanding of both God and humanity. When the grace of God flows into my life, the Holy Spirit is the divine messenger. When the voice of God wakes me from a sound sleep, the Holy Spirit speaks the words that rouse me to a different level of awareness of my God and of myself. The Holy Spirit infuses my being with a transforming quality, a quality not easily framed in verbal language. The Holy Spirit moves in the marrow of the bones, even as it illumines the mind. It comes like a bird that flies free from the heart, but it may also be a lion that stalks out of the brain.

The Bible is the authoritative source of my understanding of God. My Christianity is enhanced and enriched by the influence of the Judaism of the Old Testament. I worship the God of the Old Testament, even as I embrace the Jesus of the New Testament. I believe that Jesus embodies a fulfillment of the prophecies of the Old Testament; through Jesus my vision of God is enlarged to encompass the totality of the Scriptures. I believe the Holy Spirit empowered those who wrote the text. The passionate and powerful stories which comprise the Text brim with a richness and authenticity that reassures me that my imperfection can be brought to the same God who is the dynamic force in the canon.

Bibliography

Ashley, David & David Michael Orenstein. *Sociological Theory: Classical Statements*. Newton: Allyn & Bacon, Inc., 1985.

Baroja, Julio Caro. *The World of Witches*. Chicago: University of Chicago Press, 1965.

Baxter, Sandra and Marjorie Lansing. *Women and Politics*. Ann Arbor: The University of Michigan Press, 1980.

Bloom, Harold & David Rosenburg. *The Book of J.* New York: Grove Weidenfeld, 1990.

Brown, Peter R. L. *The Body and Society: Men, Women, and Sexual Renunciation in Early Christianity*. New York: Columbia University Press, 1988.

Brownrigg, Ronald. *Who's Who in the New Testament.*
New York: Crown Publishing Co., 1971.

Brueggemann, Walter. *Genesis.* Atlanta: John Knox
Press, 1982.

Burris, Virginia. *Chastity as Autonomy.* Lewiston: The
Edwin Mellen Press, 1987.

Bynum, Caroline Walker. "'... And Woman His Humanity': Female Imagery in the Religious Writing of
the Later Middle Ages." in *Gender and Religion:
On the Complexity of Symbols.* Edited by Caroline Walker Bynum, Steven Harrell, and Paula
Richman, Boston: Beacon Press, 1986.

Bynum, Caroline Walker, quoted in Ann Loades.
Searching for Lost Coins. Allison Park: Pickwick
Publications, 1987.

Calvin, John. *Institutes of the Christian Religion.* Vol 1,
Edited by John T. McNeill, and translated by
Ford Lewis Battles, Philadelphia: The West-
minster Press, 1960.

Carey, Archbishop of Canterbury George. *Monday
Morning: A Magazine for Presbyterian Leaders.* 58,
no. 1 (January 11, 1993): 23.

Carmody, Denise Lardner. *Biblical Woman: Contemporary Reflections on Scriptural Texts.* New York:
Crossroad Publishing Co., 1988.

Childe, V. Gordon. *The Dawn of European Civilization.*
New York: Alfred A. Knopf, 1958.

Cohen, A. *Everyman's Talmud.* New York: Schocken
Books, 1975.

"Confession of Faith, The Westminster," *The Book of
Confessions.* Louisville: Presbyterian Church,
U.S.A., 1991-92.

Deen, Edith. *All the Women of the Bible.* San Francisco: Harper and Row Publishers, 1955.

Diagnostic and Statistical Manual of Mental Disorders. 3rd Ed. Revised, Washington, D.C.: American Psychiatric Association, 1987.

Dourley, John P. *The Illness That We Are: A Jungian Critique of Christianity.* Toronto: Inner City Books, 1984.

Dourley, John P. *The Psyche as Sacrament: A Comparative Study of C. G. Jung and Paul Tillich.* Toronto: Inner City Books, 1981.

Durang, Christopher, quoted in Arthur W. Frank. "Anger, Illness, and Healing," *Second Opinion,* 17, no. 4 (April 1992): 11-19.

Edinger, Edward F. *The Christian Archetype: A Jungian Commentary on the Life of Christ.* Toronto: Inner City Books, 1987.

Eisler, Riane. *The Chalice and the Blade.* San Francisco: Harper and Row, 1987.

Estés, Clarissa Pinkola. *Women Who Run With The Wolves: Myths and Stories of the Wild Woman Archetype.* New York: Ballantine Books, 1992.

Fallon, J. E. "St. Mary Magdalene" *New Catholic Encyclopedia,* Vol. 9, New York: McGraw Hill, 1967.

Fallows, Samuel, ed. *Bible Encyclopedia and Scriptural Dictionary.* Chicago: Howard Severance Co., 1911.

Fiorenza, Elisabeth Schüssler. *Bread Not Stone: The Challenge of Feminist Biblical Interpretation.* Boston: Beacon Press, 1984.

Fiorenza, Elisabeth Schüssler. *In Memory of Her: A Feminist Theological Reconstruction of Christian Origins.* New York: Crossroad Publishing, 1985.

Fiorenza, Elisabeth Schüssler. "Response to the 'Social Functions of Women's Asceticism in the Roman East,' by Antoinette Clark Wire." in *Images of the Feminine in Gnosticism.* edited by Karen L. King, Philadelphia: Fortress Press, 1988.

Fortune, Marie M. *Is Nothing Sacred?* San Francisco: Harper San Francisco, 1989.

Fox, Matthew, ed. *Western Spirituality: Historical Roots, Ecumenical Routes.* Notre Dame: Fides/Claretian, 1979.

Gibran, Kahlil. *The Garden of the Prophet.* New York: Alfred A. Knopf, 1982.

Gibran, Kahlil. *The Prophet.* New York: Alfred A. Knopf, 1983.

Gibran, Kahlil. *Sand and Foam.* New York: Alfred A. Knopf, 1981.

Gibran, Kahlil. *Secrets of the Heart.* New York: Signet Books, 1947.

Gibran, Kahlil. *Spiritual Sayings of Kahlil Gibran.* Secaucus: The Citadel Press, 1962.

Gibran, Kahlil. *A Tear and a Smile.* Translated by H. M. Nahmad. New York: Alfred A. Knopf, 1950.

Gibran, Kahlil. *The Wanderer: His Parables and Sayings.* New York: Alfred A. Knopf, 1981.

Gimbutas, Marija. *The Early Civilizations of Europe: A Monograph for IndoEuropean Studies.* Los Angeles: University of California Press, 1980.

González, Justo. *The Story of Christianity.* San Francisco: Harper and Row Publishers, 1984.

Guthrie, W. K. C. *The Greeks and Their Gods.* Boston: Beacon Press, 1955.

Harris, Lis. *Holy Days: The World of a Hasidic Family.* New York: Macmillan Publishing Co., 1985.

Harris, Maria. *Women and Teaching.* New York: Paulist Press, 1988.

Hosmer, Rachel. *Gender & God: Love and Desire in Christian Spirituality.* Cambridge, Mass.: Cowley Publications, 1986.

Hymowitz, Carol and Michael Weissman. *A History of Women in America.* New York: Bantam, 1978.

Julian of Norwich. *Julian of Norwich: Showings.* Translated by Edmund College and James Walsh, New York: Paulist Press, 1978.

Jung, Carl Gustav. *Man and His Symbols.* San Sebastian, Spain: Ferguson Publishing Co., 1964.

Jung, Carl Gustav. *Modern Man in Search of a Soul.* New York: Harcourt Brace Jovanovich, 1933.

King, Karen L., ed. *Images of the Feminine in Gnosticism.* Philadelphia: Fortress Press, 1988.

Kümmel, Werner Georg. *Introduction to the New Testament.* Translated by Howard Clark Kee, Nashville: Abingdon Press, 1973.

Lane, William L. *The Gospel According to Mark.* Grand Rapids, Mich.: Wm. B. Eerdmans Publishing Co., 1974.

Leander of Seville, quoted in Rosemary Radford Ruether. *Sexism and God Talk.* Boston: Beacon Press, 1983.

Leonard, Linda Schierse. *The Wounded Woman: Healing the Father-Daughter Relationship.* Boston: Shambhala, 1985.

Leonard, Linda Schierse. *On the Way to the Wedding: Transforming the Love Relationship.* Boston: Shambhala, 1986.

Loades, Ann. *Searching for Lost Coins.* Allison Park: Pickwick Publications, 1987.

Luther, Martin, quoted in Amaury Riencourt. *Sex and Power in History.* New York: Dell Publishing Co., 1974.

Map, Walter quoted in Elizabeth Stanton. *The Original Feminist Attack on the Bible.* New York: Arno Press, 1974.

McLintock, John and James Strong, eds. *Encyclopedia of Biblical, Theological, and Ecclesiastical Literature. 1873,* Grand Rapids: Baker Book House, reprint 1969.

Moltmann-Wendel, Elisabeth. *The Women Around Jesus.* New York: Crossroad Publishing Co., 1980.

Moltmann-Wendel, Elisabeth and Jürgen Moltmann. *Humanity in God.* New York: The Pilgrim Press, 1983.

Moore, Robert. "Healing the Masculine," Lecture delivered at the C. G. Jung Institute in Chicago, 1991.

Morrison, Clinton. *An Analytical Concordance to the Revised Standard Version of the New Testament.* Philadelphia: The Westminster Press, 1979.

The New Oxford Annotated Bible. New York: Oxford University Press, 1962.

The New Revised Standard Version of the Holy Bible. Nashville: Thomas Nelson, Inc., 1989.

The New Revised Standard Version of the Holy Bible. Nashville: Cokesbury, 1990.

Norton, Mary Beth, et. al. *A People and a Nation,* 2nd. Ed. Boston: Houghton Mifflin Co., 1986.

Ostling, Richard N. "Gay Rabbis: Toppling An Ancient Tradition," *Time,* (July 9, 1990): 62.

Order, The Book of. Presbyterian Church, U.S.A., Louisville: 1991-92.

Pagels, Elaine. *The Gnostic Gospels.* New York: Random House, 1979.

Peterson, Michael, quoted by Jason Berry. *Lead Us Not Into Temptation.* New York: Doubleday, 1992.

Rendel, Margherita, ed. *Women, Power and Political Systems.* New York: St. Martins Press, 1981.

Robinson, James, ed. *The Nag Hammadi Library in English.* San Francisco: Harper and Row Publishers, 1988.

Romano, Catherine, "A Psycho-Spiritual History of Teresa of Avila: A Woman's Perspective." in *Western Spirituality: Historical Roots, Ecumenical Routes.* edited by Matthew Fox, Notre Dame: Fides/Claretian, 1979.

Ruether, Rosemary Radford. *Sexism and God-Talk.* Boston: Beacon Press, 1983.

Ruether, Rosemary Radford. *Womenguides, Readings Toward a Feminist Theology.* Boston: Beacon Press, 1985.

Saint Augustine. *Confessions.* New York: Viking Penguin Inc., 1961.

Saint John Chrysostom, quoted in Bernard Murstein. *Love, Sex and Marriage Through the Ages.* New York: Springer Publishing Co., 1974.

Sanford, John. *Evil: The Shadow Side of Reality.* New York: Crossroad, 1981.

Sanford, John. *Healing Body and Soul: The Meaning of Illness in the New Testament and in Psychotherapy.* Louisville: Westminster John Knox Press, 1992.

Schaberg, Jane. *The Illegitimacy of Jesus: A Feminist Theological Interpretation of the Infancy Narratives.* New York: Crossroad, 1990.

Scholem, Gershom. *Kabbalah.* New York: Dorset Press, 1987.

Schweizer, Eduard. *The Good News According to Mark.* Translated by Donald H. Madvig, Atlanta: John Knox Press, 1970.

Soranus. *Gynaecia.* Edited by J. Ilberg, Leipsig: Teub-
ner, 1927. English Translation: Temkin, O.
Soranus' Gynaecology. Baltimore: Johns Hopkins
University Press, 1956.

Spong, Bishop John Shelby. *Born of a Woman: A Bishop
Rethinks the Birth of Jesus.* San Francisco: Harper
San Francisco, 1992.

Spong, Bishop John Shelby. *Rescuing the Bible from
Fundamentalism: A Bishop Rethinks The Meaning
of Scripture.* San Francisco: Harper San Francisco, 1991.

Stone, Merlin. *When God Was A Woman.* New York:
Harcourt Brace Jovanovich, 1976.

Tetlow, Elisabeth Meier. *Women and Ministry in the
New Testament.* Lanham: University Press of
America, Inc., 1980.

Theological Dictionary of the New Testament. Vols. 3 &
4, edited by Gerhard Kittel, and translated and
edited by Geoffrey W. Bromley, Grand Rapids,
Mich.: Wm. B. Eerdmans Publishing Co., 1965.

Turville-Petre, E. O. G. *Myth and Religion.* New York:
Holt, Rinehart and Winston, 1964.

Ulanov, Ann Bedford. *The Feminine in Jungian Psychology and in Christian Theology.* Evanston: Northwestern University Press, 1971.

Ulanov, Ann Bedford. *The Wisdom of the Psyche,*
Cambridge: Cowley Publications, 1988.

Warner, Marina. *Alone of All Her Sex: The Myth and
The Cult of The Virgin Mary.* New York: Vintage
Books, 1976.

Westermann, Claus. *Genesis 1-11: A Commentary.*
Translated by John J. Scullion (S.J.) Minneapolis: Augsburg Publishing House, 1984.

Whitmont, Edward C. *Return of the Goddess.* New York: The Crossroad Publishing Co., 1982.

Woodman, Marion. *Addiction to Perfection: The Still Unravished Bride.* Toronto: Inner City Books, 1982.

Woodman, Marion. *Leaving My Father's House: A Journey to Conscious Femininity.* Boston: Shambhala Publications, 1993.

Woodman, Marion. *The Owl Was a Baker's Daughter: Obesity, Anorexia Nervosa and the Repressed Feminine.* Toronto: Inner City Books, 1980

Woodman, Marion. *The Pregnant Virgin: A Process of Psychological Transformation.* Toronto: Inner City Books, 1985.

Index

Abraham, 25
Achievement orientation,
    36
Acts, 44
Adam, 27
Aelred of Rievaulx, 57
Alcoholics, closet, 31
Algonquin, 30
Amazon, armored, 124
Andrew, 53, 117
Anger, 2-3, 5, 52-53, 84-
    86, 88, 117, 143, 173,
    179, 183

Anima, 7, 11-12
Animus, 7-8, 11-12
Anorexic(s), 123, 169
Apatheia, 104
Aphrodite, 18
Archetypal patterns. *See*
    Patterns, archetypal
Archetype(s), 120-24,
    129-44, 149-51, 156,
    162, 174
Archetypes of: King,
    131-34, 139; Lover,
    131, 135-36;

Archetypes, cont'd.:
Magus or Magician,
131, 134-35; Warrior,
131-34
Artemis, 17
Ascetic(s), 100, 102, 104,
107-25
Ashur, 19
Assumptions, cultural, 14,
17, 65-67, 76, 85, 91-
92
Athena, 17
Augustine, 46, 102, 104
Authoritarianism, 5, 11,
16, 31, 90
Authority, 67, 69, 75, 83,
89

Basil of Caesarea, 108
Battle of the Little Big
Horn, 30
Battle of the Rosebud, 30
Bethany, Mary of, 45-46,
49
Body, physical, 1, 18, 51-
55, 57, 79, 84-85, 91,
97, 100-101, 104-5,
108-10, 112-14, 118,
122-25, 142, 148-49,
152, 154, 158, 161,
163, 166, 169-74, 179
Body language, 79, 155
Book of Order, 71, 164
Bridegroom, divine, 109

British Common Law,
33-34
Brown, Peter R. L., 103-
5
Bulimia, 23
Bultmann, Rudolf, 63-
64
Bynum, Caroline Walk-
er, 57, 112

Calvin, John, 152
Campbell, Joseph, 81,
83
Cana, marriage at, 149
Candidate under care,
71-74, 76, 78, 80-84
Canon, 13, 20, 24, 25,
27, 51-54, 56-58, 65,
71, 92, 101, 114-15,
132, 135-36, 139-
40, 142, 144, 148-
50, 173, 180
Carey George, Arch-
bishop of Canter-
bury, 89-90
Catherine of Siena, 122
Chagall, Marc, 1-2
Cheyenne, 30
Childe, V. Gordon, 16
Christ, 1, 20, 28, 44-48,
51-52, 54-59, 63-65,
88, 91, 109-12, 118,
157-58
Christian Apologists, 44,
54, 56

Christianity, 2, 26, 47, 54, 56, 63, 65, 72, 80, 86, 88-90, 97-105, 108, 116-18, 121-22, 131-36, 141-44, 161, 163, 170, 178

Chrysostom, John, 29, 46

Church, 1, 2, 4-6, 10-13, 23, 27-28, 35-37, 44-46, 48, 66, 71, 74, 76, 78-90, 92, 97-105, 109-16, 118-19, 123, 130-43, 148, 150-53, 155, 164-66, 169-74, 181-84

Clement of Alexandria, 99

Clergy, 3, 37, 66, 71-72, 76, 79-81, 84-88, 90, 136, 138, 140-43, 150, 153, 165, 173

Clockwork Orange, 76

Cofitachique, Lady of, 30

Collective unconscious, 13, 18, 120, 131, 137, 148, 150, 156, 168, 170

Committee on Preparation, 71-78, 132

Criticism, historical-literary, 4

Crook, General George, 30

Demons, 47-48, 99

Denomination, 2-3, 12-13, 29, 67, 71, 76, 78, 80-81, 83, 153, 181-83

Depression, 3; manic, 47-48

D'Etaples, Jacque Lefevre, 45

Distortion, 4, 6, 10, 35, 52, 54, 63, 65, 71, 98-99, 116, 120, 123-24, 130-31, 154, 163, 168-69, 172

Durang, Christopher, 84

Egalitarian, 2, 13-14, 16, 19, 27

Eisler, Riane, 13, 15-16

Epileptic, 47

Eve, 27, 43

Exegesis, 4

Ex nihilo, 180

Explicit Curriculum, 67, 70

Fathers of the Church, 21, 44, 88, 99, 155, 170

Feminine, 7, 10-12, 15, 19, 23, 100, 103, 112-13, 118, 123, 154, 158, 161, 164, 166-69, 174

Feminist, 66, 71, 85, 121

Fiorenza, Elisabeth Schüssler, 54, 58, 118
Food deprivation, 118, 122
Frank, Arthur, 85

Gender(s), 12, 15, 19, 23-25, 29, 32-33, 35, 37, 71, 80-81, 98, 100-101, 104, 120, 122, 130, 154, 161, 163, 178
Gibran, Kahlil, 1, 9, 43, 63, 97, 107, 129, 147, 161, 177
Gimbutas, Marija, 13-16
Gnostic, gospels of: the Egyptians, 117; Mary, 53-54, 59, 117, 148; Philip, 51-52; Thomas 52, 100, 117; Pistis Sophia, 117
God, 11, 13, 19, 27-28, 30, 32, 43, 55-56, 59, 70, 76, 80, 83-84, 87, 91-92, 98, 100, 102-5, 110-11, 113-15, 130, 133-43, 161-63, 180-87
God as Father, 162-63
God as Mother, 111-13, 161-63
Goddess, 13, 17-21, 23, 163, 166-67

Goddess, Mother, 18
Gospels, in the canon: John, 44, 53, 55-57, 88; Luke, 47, 50, 52, 55; Mark, 44, 47, 52, 54, 56, 151; Matthew, 49, 52, 55
Greek Orthodox Church, 46
Gregory the Great, Pope, 46
Gregory of Nyssa, 108
Grief, 3, 5, 77, 84, 178, 182-83

Habits of the mind, 18-20, 22, 28-29, 37, 90-91, 119-20, 161, 163
Harris, Lis, 25, 98
Harris, Maria, 66-71
Hasidic Jews, 24-25, 98
Hebrew, language of: 70, 76, 113-16
Hebrews, 20, 26, 99
Hellenistic, influence, 101-2, 136, 143, 174
Hera, 17
Heresy as spiritual treason, 88
Heretical sources, 51, 54, 102, 104
Historical Transformation, 13
Hitler, Adolf, 132

Holy Spirit, 113, 162, 164, 170
Holy Spirit Mother, Christ as: 111-13
Holy Wars, 133
Household goddess, 34
Hubris, 150
Hussein, Sadam, 132
Hutchinson, Anne Marbury, 32

Icon, 10, 138
Image of God, 13, 80, 103, 112, 136,
Imagery, female, 18, 113, 122-23
Images, matriarchal, 16, 65
Implicit curriculum, 67-70
Indian tribes, 29-31
Individuation, 131, 151
Industrial age, 33
Initiation, 12, 81-83
Inquirer stage, 71
Iranaeus, 45

"J," 116
Jerome, 104
Jesus, 1, 44-45, 47-49, 51-52, 54-55, 58-59, 63-65, 78, 86-87, 91, 98, 100-102, 107, 112, 115, 117, 129-44,

Jesus, cont'd., 147-53, 156-57, 162-64, 167, 172-73
Judeo-Christian, 19, 65, 90
Julian of Norwich, 110-12, 116
Jung, Carl G., 6-7, 9-10, 18, 23, 68-69, 119-20, 154-55

Kabbalism, 113, 118, 180-81
Kunkel, Fritz, 68-69
Künstle, Karl, 46

Labyrinth, Malekulaian, 45
Leander of Seville, 103
Levi, 53
Libidinal energy, 155-56
Literal translationists, 27, 29, 77, 88, 132, 151, 163
Lover, Christ as: 109
Luther, Martin, 21-22, 29, 78-79

Macrina, 107-10
Magdalene, Mary, 10, 37, 43-59, 63-66, 78, 91-92, 100, 130, 136, 147-51, 156-58, 167, 172-74, 184

Magdalene Spirit, 167, 174
Male dominance, 3, 20, 36, 65, 91
Map, Walter, 29
Marduk, 19
Marriage, 148-49, 153
Mary, the Virgin, 44, 57, 107, 121-22, 138, 162
Masculine, 7-8, 11-13, 15, 20, 23, 123-24, 131, 163, 169
Mask (persona) of Christianity, 141-42
Matrilineal, 16
Matter, 10-11
Mayflower Compact, 31
Mclintock, John, 43
Mellaart, James, 13
Men, 10, 20, 22, 25-27, 33, 36-37, 56, 71-72, 75, 88, 91, 98, 100, 103, 130-31, 138-40, 150, 154, 156, 168-69, 178
Menstruation, 24-26
Mesopotamia, 20
Midrashim, 4
Mikvah, 25-26, 98
Ministry of the Word and Sacrament, 12, 71, 79, 168
Misogyny, 63-78, 84, 86, 92

Moltmann-Wendel, Elisabeth, 45-46, 50
Moore, Robert, 131, 133,
Morality, 140
Moral Theology, 67
Mother Earth, 11
Mysterion, 64-65, 80, 82, 113, 121, 137, 174
Mysterium tremendum, 152
Mystery, 64-65, 134, 137, 156, 163-64
Mystery cults, 82

Nag Hammadi, 117
Neolithic art, 15-16
Nephesh, 114-15, 181
New Revised Standard Version, 13, 56
Norms, cultural, 7, 16, 19, 23, 67, 85, 90-92, 119, 167
Null curriculum, 67-70
Numinosity, 9-10, 12, 59, 65, 170

Ordination, 12, 71, 73, 76, 78-79, 81, 83, 85, 168-69, 184
Origen, 45, 105

Pagels, Elaine, 51-52
Passionate penitent, 46-49

Patriarchy, 11-13, 15, 65, 71, 87, 90-92, 105, 116, 129, 132, 142-43, 149, 169, 178-80, 184

Patterns: archetypal, 18-19, 22, 29, 36-37, 43, 49, 72, 79, 100, 120-24, 129-44, 147, 150-51, 153-54, 162, 174, 183; Demographic gender, 37; Patriarchal, 11-13, 15, 65, 71, 87, 90-92, 129, 132, 142-43, 173

Paul, St., the Apostle, 18, 27-29, 55, 102,

Pentateuch, 116

Peter, 52-55, 57, 117

Phallic potency, 131-32

Pharisee(s), 28, 48, 135

Polarity, 154-57

Political efficacy, 36

Power, 11-12, 15-18, 20, 27, 29, 31, 33-36, 54, 56, 67, 72, 75, 81-82, 84, 86, 90, 112, 122, 129-32, 134-36, 138, 151-52, 169, 173, 179-80

Presbyterian Church, U.S.A., 12, 76, 80-81, 155, 181-82

Presbytery, 71-79, 81

Projection(s), 20-21, 37, 43, 46-47, 49-50, 57, 59, 66, 72-75, 77-87, 100, 120, 123, 130, 134, 136, 138-40, 142-43, 147, 151-54, 162, 171-72, 184

Promiscuity, 136

Psyche, 7-8, 18, 31, 35-37, 119-24, 130-31, 136-37, 139, 151, 154, 156, 179

Puritans, 31-32

Qadishtu, 98-99

Rabbi(s), 58, 147-48

Rape, 21, 36, 168

Revelation of God, 55

Ruether, Rosemary Radford, 17, 109

Russell, Letty, 67

Sabbath, 26

Sacrament, 12, 48, 132, 153

Sacred, 23, 25-26, 98-99, 105, 112-13, 138-39, 142, 150, 153, 161-66, 174, 180-82

Sanford, John, 141

Satan, 151

Scapegoat, 47, 173

Schweitzer, Albert, 63-64

Secret (sacred), 131, 138-39, 142-43, 148-50, 153, 181-82

Sexual harassment, 143, 168

Sexual indiscretions, 48

Sexual intercourse, 26, 98-100, 138-39, 154

Sexuality, 3-4, 10, 20, 37, 43, 46, 49-50, 70, 97, 99-100, 104, 110, 114, 118, 122, 132, 136, 143, 148, 150, 155-56, 161, 163, 170-74, 184

Sexual Practices, 21

Shadow, 7-8, 12, 78-79, 120, 132-36, 141, 150-53, 156, 172-73, 182

Shekhinah, 113, 180

Societies: goddess worshiping, 13, 19, 21, 23; warrior, 13, 15-17, 20

Society, Varna, 15

Son of God, 90

Son of Man, 164

Son of Woman, 164

Soranus, 100

Soul, 1, 5, 8, 11-12, 17-18, 48, 57, 64, 69, 81, 85, 102-3, 107, 113-14, 117, 121, 124, 133, 140, 143, 157,

Soul, cont'd., 161-62, 164-66, 168-74, 178, 181-82, 185-87

Spain, 109

Spirit, 2-3, 11, 18, 27, 30, 64, 72, 100-103, 112-14, 123, 142-43, 149, 151, 157, 181

Spirituality, 3-4, 10, 20, 59, 90, 101, 110, 115, 119, 122, 124, 184

Spong, Bishop John Shelby, 149

Stalin, Joseph, 132

Status quo, 13

Stereotypical sinful woman, 46, 48

Stone, Merlin, 19-20, 98

Stratification, gender, 24

Sumer, 17, 84

Talmud, The, 23-25, 99

Teresa of Avila, 109-10

Tertullian, 86-87

Theology, feminist, 66

Theology, liberation, 87

Theology, reformed, 71, 130, 181

Torah, The, 25

Traitor, 87-89, 91

Trible, Phyllis, 70

Trinity, 111-12, 162, 167, 169-70, 172

Ulanov, Anne Belford, 154-56, 166
Unconscious 2, 7-8, 12-14, 17-19, 21, 23, 29, 35-37, 44, 46, 49, 52, 56, 65-66, 70, 72, 74, 79-83, 85-87, 90-92, 101, 119-24, 131, 134, 136-43, 148, 150-56, 162, 168-70, 179
Unconscious, collective. *See* Collective unconscious
Unconscious, personal, 7, 119
United States, 29, 31, 33, 35

Veblen, Thorstein, 6, 18, 22, 119-20
Victorian, 34
Virgin, 17, 21, 26, 105, 107, 115, 121-23
Virginity, 26, 97, 103, 105, 115-23

Whore, 47, 79, 121, 123, 138, 153
Widow(s), 27, 108
Winthrop, John, 32

Woman/women, 1-6, 8, 10, 14, 16, 18-20, 21, 25, 27-37, 43-59, 67-91, 97-105, 107-23, 130-31, 137-43, 148-58, 162-74, 178-84
Word of God, 91-92

Yugoslavia, 168

Zeus, 18

About the Author

SANDRA M. RUSHING is an Ordained Minister in the Presbyterian Church, U.S.A. She is the author of a book of poetry, *Essence of Autumn*, and an award-winning sociological study entitled "The Economics of Gender Stratification" (1988).

ISBN 0-89789-388-3

90000>
EAN
9 780897 893886

HARDCOVER BAR CODE